M000267752

THE

INDEX

COL

SAGA OF
SWEETHEART

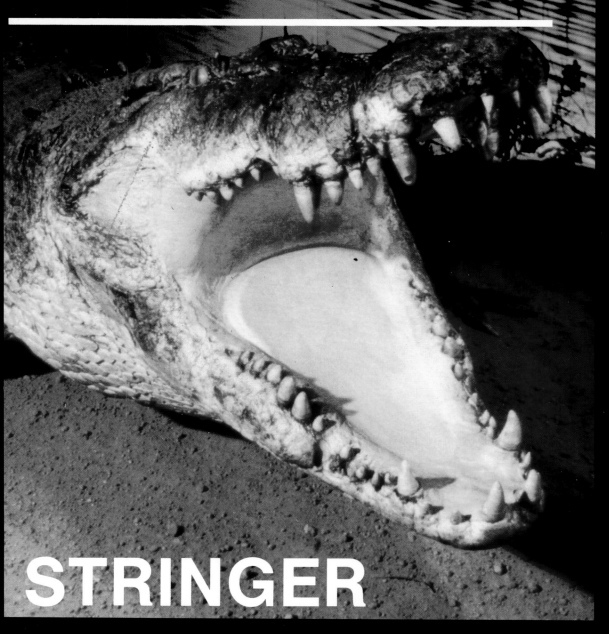

STRINGER

This soft cover edition is an exclusive
production published in 1999
by J.B. Books Pty Ltd
P.O. Box 118
Marleston 5033 South Australia
Phone/Fax (08) 8297 1669
First published in hard cover in 1986
By Adventure Publications
Darwin.

All rights reserved. No part of this
publication may be reproduced,
stored or transmitted in any form
or by any means, electronic,
mechanical, photocopying, recording
or otherwise without written
permission of the publisher.

ISBN 1 876622 02 4

© Col Stringer

Produced by Phoenix Offset

Printed in Hong Kong

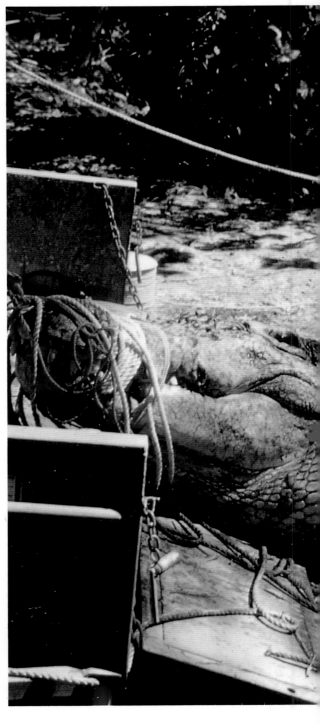

ACKNOWLEDGEMENTS

The author and publishers would like to express
their gratitude to the following people for their
valuable assistance in producing this book.

The author's wife, Jan Stringer

Dave Lindner	Jacko
N.T. Museum	Boyne Litchfield
N.T. News	Max Sargent
Dept of Chief Minister N.T.	Greg Biddell
Nuggett Marjar	Clyde Reborse
Denver Marchant	Ray Petherick
Ken Phillips	Max Curtain
George Haritos	Ian Watson
The Melbourne Sun	Brian Cowan
State Reference Library	Carl Blumanis

Photo courtesy Dave Lindner

JB BOOKS

J.B. BOOKS AUSTRALIA

FOREWORD

by

Col Stringer

Few crocodiles ever develop into maneaters. Most crocs are content to be left alone and as they only have to eat perhaps once a week, the big amphibians' reputation may have been painted blacker than they really deserve. However make no mistake about it, crocodiles are dangerous and deserve healthy respect. They are the most dangerous of all creatures when in their natural environment, fearing nothing at all, except man. Maybe their curiosity is aroused by him.

In my research for this book I found some of the following attacks.

* Roper River early 1900's - 2 white men asleep in their boat, one with his foot over the side, a sudden shriek and he disappeared into the water.

* Aboriginal man taken by large croc in Daly River left wedged under tree root at the bottom of the river, regained consciousness, swam out to safety.

* Aboriginal man attacked in Darwin Harbour - seized in jaws - wriggled around - stuck his fingers in its eyes - broke free - dived to bottom and swam back to boat. Croc consequently attacked the boat.

Photo Haust Faustmann

* 1890's Government Surveyor had blankets pulled from his hammock by huge croc.

Even in recent years attacks and fatalaties have been increasing as the saurians numbers recover.

Crocs play an important part in the balance of the north's eco-system, from offshore islands and mainland coasts to inland waterways and billabongs. While water is their main domain, crocs do travel overland, especially when waterholes dry up. In fact, they may range miles from rivers or waterholes, usually at night, sensing water at vast distances. Wherever sufficient water, fresh or salt, and sufficient large prey exists, crocodiles occur.

Crocs are territorial and will defend their territory against 'invaders' of their own species. They are also particularly dangerous during the breeding season (Wet Season and preceeding build up weather) and as in the case of Sweetheart, most attacks take place during this time. During the breeding season they may prove intolerant of other large animals, including man.

The big saurians can stalk their victim virtually undetected underwater without so much as a ripple betraying their presence. The bulk of the body is kept beneath the surface of the water, unobserved with just nostrils (on the top of the snout) and its knob like eyes above the water in order to see and breathe. When close enough to the intended victim it shoots forward to seize the drinking animal by the snout or leg. Crocs can remain submerged for long periods of time and despite popular belief are very fast on land as well as in the water. The big reptiles are remarkably agile - able to propel their bodies clear of the water in the pursuit of food. An attacking crocodile is a formidable foe - an awesome, terrifying spectacle - able to strike fear into the heart of the bravest. Certainly Sweetheart must hold that record. Even to the most imaginative, the true saga of Sweetheart provides an exciting account of adventure and misadventure.

Man has always been fascinated with creatures capable of 'fighting back' so to speak, to challange his supremacy on this planet. Books and movies such as "Jaws", "King Kong" and "Grizzly" are but a few - but truth is stranger than fiction.

Here in the Northern Territory the name has almost become legend with thousands filing past annually to view the huge mounted body in the Darwin Museum.

For many years, probably most of the 1900's, Sweetheart made his home on a remote stretch of the Finniss River, a beautiful and outwardly serene billabong known as Sweets. From early accounts we find the aboriginals of that area knew of this big croc. Later on Sweetheart made his presence convincingly known to all who stumbled across his path from station owner to croc hunters. However it appears Sweetheart was content to co-exist with mankind until the 1960's - then something unexplainable but certainly dramatic happend that forever changed the giant croc into a rogue. From then on Sweetheart carried out a seemingly personal vendetta against the boats and motors that plied his home waterhole - a vendetta that without exception saw him the victor of every encounter until his capture and death in 1979.

What happened to this huge croc to turn him into a rogue remains a mystery - but for many years Sweetheart was something of an inevitable celebrity, hideous to his victims but fascinating to his armchair supporters, attracting media attention and gross inevitable exaggerations from all around the world. Take the newspaper article from Great Britain! After one attack where he succceeded in attacking and overturning a boat with two fishermen aboard, headlines screamed "Giant croc attacks boat, swallows outboard motor". Reporters and television camera teams made the long journey north, anxious to shoot the story of the year - Sweetheart's demise.

When we set out to document this story, we had little idea it would take us two years to compile. It has lead us to men and women right across the nation, men and women of all walks of life who have experienced first hand the wrath of a "Sweetheart embrace". Folks like Nugget Marjar who grew up just a short distance from Sweetheart's lair, Ray Petherick the old croc shooter, American station owner Clyde Reborse, Boyne Litchfield (the first recognised attack victim), Dave Lindner, the wildlife ranger who staked himself out as "bait" to entice the croc to attack his boat. It was Dave who pieced together much of the puzzle and eventually captured the huge croc. Probably he knows more about Sweetheart, in his period of notoriety than any man alive.

Was Sweetheart just an isolated rogue croc venting his wrath on aluminium boats that ventured into his home lair? Was he an innocent victim who was painfully wounded by rifle or boat and sought revenge? Was he simply defending his "harem" of lady crocs and offspring against the intrusion of what he mistakenly felt were rival lovers? Or were the attacks carried out by more than one croc with Sweetheart "wearing" the total blame?

Believe me, the story is a fascinating one - one of which we will never know the complete truth.

This is the legend of a rogue croc extrodinaire - the most infamous crocodile in history - victor in battle over at least ten encounters with boats and motors.

This then is the untold Saga of Sweetheart!

Photo courtesy N.T.News

INTRODUCTION

by

Dave Lindner

The saga of Sweetheart, or that part of it that earned him a permanent place in Territory history, could only have occurred in the nineteen seventies.

The seventies were a critical period for survival for Australian crocodiles, particularly the larger species whose imposing record as a predator, a maneater at that, left him out of the protection afforded the harmless freshwater species granted in the mid sixties.

Sweetheart went on the rampage during the period of greatest upsurge in sporting barramundi fishing, during a period of uncertainty in crocodile control but also during a period of idealism in wildlife conservation.

The experts were dealing with an endangered species, not a maneater. If a crocodile ate a man it could be an unfortunate and unintentional mistake on the croc's part.

Territorians would have to drop all water recreation to give the croc a go and also stop calling them 'gators please, apart from being scientifically wrong it has a rather savage sound about it.

During the seventies crocodiles were officially gentled to support the protection management policies. Fishermen on the other hand, like all true sportsmen, are one-eyed in pursuit of their recreation and as many Territorians of the fair sex could sadly testify, there's just no time for Sweethearts when the barra are biting.

DAVE LINDNER

Photo courtesy N.T.News - Dave skinning
Sweetheart

THE BIG LIZARDS

by

Tom Cole

Maneaters there certainly are, I was involved with one myself at a place called Marshall Lagoon in New Guinea. According to the records, which were by no means complete, it had taken seventeen people.

At the request of the Administration I went to Marshall Lagoon and succeeded in trapping it, and although there are records of individual fatalities, I have never heard of one before or since that approached these figures which were well substantiated.

It must be remembered that when a crocodile makes it's initial foray into the human area for its food supply and selects Europeans, it's life expectancy immediately becomes limited, but not necessarily so should its victim happen to be a pagan savage whose superstitions and totems frequently embrace what amounts to a veneration of the crocodile.

Following my success in killing the maneater of Marshall Lagoon, it was with some regret that I was unable to follow it up with a demonstration of walking on water.

The name alligator is a corruption of El Lagarto, which is Spanish for lizard, while the origin of crocodile is similar but of far greater antiquity. The followers of Herodatus, on seeing these creatures in the Nile, called them Krokodeilos because of their similarity to the lizards of their homeland.

Among the last of the prehistoric animals, twenty one different species are known to scientists who believe that they have been around for something like two hundred million years, which is quite a while. Of these Australia hosts two.

One, a harmless fish eating variety which grows to a length of four or five feet, known as the Johnstone River, or Johnstonian crocodile, and is essentially a denizen of freshwater streams. The other, a massive brute which, in rare cases, may grow to a length of twenty feet and is known to men of letters as Crocodylus Porosus.

Although both are true crocodiles, the larger saltwater animal has always been known to bushmen of the north as an alligator. This is partly ignorance and partly to differentiate it from its freshwater cousin the Johnstonian, which was always called a crocodile.

To perpetuate the confusion there are three rivers in the Northern Territory where the saltwater variety have always been plentiful, named the West Alligator, the South Alligator and the East Alligator. From Queensland across to Western Australia there is a liberal sprinkling of Alligator Creeks, there is an Alligator Lagoon and an Alligator Swamp, but no alligators, the error of nomenclature is understandable.

That delightful American poet, Ogden Nash, endeavoured to put the record straight in:

THE PURIST

I give you now Professor Twist,
A conscientious scientist
Camped on a tropic riverside,
One day he missed his blushing bride.
She had, his guide informed him later,
Been eaten by an alligator,
Professor Twist could not but smile.
"You mean," he said, "a crocodile."

The Johnstone River creature is indigenous to Australia only, on the other hand the saltwater animal's habitat extends as far afield as Burma, the widest ranging of them all. Although usually referred to as a saltwater crocodile, it is equally at home in freshwater, the female going well beyond the tidal limits to deposit thirty to forty eggs in its nest, a repository to which it returns year after year.

Hidden away in a swamp, composed of bush, leaves and decayed vegetation, added to every time it returns, it is anything up to three feet in height, well above flood levels. The eggs, which are hard shelled, about the size of a goose egg, are covered with a generous layer of composted material which generates enough heat to hatch them.

When the youngsters first see the light of day they scurry to where their mother has been patiently waiting close by and off they go together. They stay with her for some time, at first feeding on her regurgitated food. But life is by no means easy for them, just about everything eats young crocodiles, including other crocodiles. But they are great survivors. I have frequently shot fully grown specimens that have lost a leg or a portion of their tail, no doubt snapped off by a predatory fish or a fellow countryman when small.

A lot of nonsense has been written and much more talked about the size to which they are supposed to grow, thirty and forty feet being freely mentioned, this I find hard to believe. I first hunted crocodile professionally in 1935 and have shot several thousand. I have been deeply involved in importing and exporting skins to large quantities, I introduced commercial hunting to New Guinea and over a long period of time I have handled in the vicinity of fifty thousand skins.

The largest crocodile I have ever shot was on the Victoria River in the Northern Territory, which measured eighteen feet nine inches. I shot one in the Kikori Delta of Papua which went eighteen foot six, another, which lived in the Gogol River until it met me, was eighteen foot three.

The largest skin I have ever seen was among a shipment which I bought from Borneo, a portion of its tail was missing but I believe that had it been complete it might have made twenty feet.

I think it's reasonable to assume that of fifty thousand skins, had any grown much longer than twenty feet, I would have seen at least one. A big crocodile is as easy to shoot as a smaller one, perhaps easier, the target is bigger.

Very little seems to be known of their life span, for the first four or five years they grow at the rate of about a foot a year, progressively slowing down, by the time they reach ten feet they are more than twenty years old. Although they are farmed commercially they are harvested long before they reach maturity, the most valuable skins being about eight or nine feet in length.

Most authorities agree that they live to a great age but no one seems to be able to put a time on it. An interesting factor which probably contributes to their longevity is that they renew their teeth, but how frequently I cannot say. I do know that an examination of the skulls of older animals reveals teeth coming away and the new ones inside the shell of the old one being discarded.

Apart from the size to which some are reported to grow quite a lot of other nonsense is talked and written about them. There is a widespread belief that their food has to be in a state of putrefaction before they eat it, but although they will certainly eat rotten flesh, their principle diet is fish which they consume as they catch them.

Another story that has gained a surprising amount of credence is that their hide will turn a bullet. It should be sufficient to dispel that story to point out that when dead the hide is removed with a knife, a sharp one certainly, further, I have never heard of a demand for crocodile hides by makers of bullet proof waistcoats.

A creature like a crocodile, because of its nature, its appearance, the kind of place it inhabits, necessarily attracts a lot of notoriety and exaggeration and the life of a crocodile hunter becomes invested with a lot of glamour, most of which, having been a hunter myself, I regret to say is unwarranted.

TOM COLE
Author of the forthcoming book "SPEARS & SMOKE SIGNALS"

Croc shooting in the 1920's here in N.T.

15

Chapter 1

THE EARLY DAYS

Nugget Marjar

It was a hot, sticky oppressive evening on the Finniss River The atmosphere was so thick and heavy one could almost taste the dampness in the air. The ever present biting, stinging mosquitos buzzed about in plague proportions, their monotonous droning the only sound to break the eerie stillness apart from the occassional shrill cry of a Curlew.

Nugget Marjar stood alert in the bow of his dugout canoe, spear poised at the ready. Slowly, nervously he wiped the trickle of sweat from his forehead, a second bead dropped onto his lips, its salty taste stinging his mouth. Nugget stood motionless, his tall, dark, muscular, naked body glistening with sweat as it reflected the brightness of the moon hovering overhead.

The scene was like a painting, serene, peaceful - the oil-like surface of the river only occassionally being disturbed by the dugout's paddle. Suddenly it appeared as though the entire river came alive, as with a frightening explosion of water, the huge, prehistoric, monstrous head of a giant crocodile broke the surface alongside Nugget's flimsy canoe.

"Old Man Sweets Lookout!" cried Nugget in amazement promptly dropping the spear and collapsing into the canoe. The crocodile lay motionless, gazing intently at the vulnerable 14 foot dugout hand hewn from the Kapok or Milkwood tree. The moon caught the wicked glint of the croc's eyes and flash of white from its formidable teeth. In a sudden swirl of water he was gone, as quickly as he had first appeared, leaving the impression that it may have never happened at all - a phantom, a figment of an overactive imagination.

Nugget and his hunting partner quietly took up their paddles and eased back to the safety of the jungle engulfed shoreline.

Possibly, just possibly this was the first recorded contact between Sweetheart and a boat. Certainly Nugget Marjar was one of the first people to make contact with the giant croc. The stage was set for what was to become one of the most exciting and for the human participants, terrifying stories in the colourful history of the Northern Territory.

Nugget was born on the Finniss River in the early 1900's and spent most of his life within a "cooee" of Sweets Lookout (Sweetheart's home billabong).

The tall aborigine, a member of the Matngala-Weret tribe, spent much of his younger years playing happily along the palm fringed river straights, diving for turtles and fishing for the giant Barramundi. However, as Nugget put it "We always give Sweets Lookout part of the river healthy respect, that was the place we all knew old Man Sweets Lookout lived". Old Man Sweets Lookout is the name the local aborigines gave to the giant croc. Strangely enough, Nugget and Sweetheart may have been born around the same time. Nugget can remember the big croc living in the waterhole for most of his life. "I started shooting crocs in late 1930's and even though there were plenty crocs, I can always remember old Man Sweets Lookout. In those days I was shooting 'gators (the name given to crocodiles in the early days) all the time. I started off getting them with a spear and later I got me a .303 rifle. The biggest croc I ever saw was an 18 footer in Sweets and a real big fella in Bullcoyne. I have been shooting 'gators right up to when they stopped in 1971. In all that time we never had any trouble with Old Man Sweets Lookout and I never ever tried to shoot him."

(I gathered from talking to Nugget, his daughters and station owners, that there developed a form of admiration for the giant croc. It was almost like a truce - the natives left the big fellow in peace - he reciprocated by not attacking them. One theory put to me by people who know the aboriginal folklore of the Sweets area (known as "Rainstone Dreaming"), is that the affinity may have been a "NGIRRWAT" (a type of totem where the aborigine actually becomes related to the animal, in this case the big crocodile, and as a result the beast is protected.) Around Sweets was "Crocodile Dreaming" country. One other view was that it may have been a "MIRR" where, if the aborigines had killed Sweetheart, some sort of punishment would befall them.

Whatever the true story, there was obviously some sort of affinity, as both parties lived in peace for years. Despite Nugget and the local aborigines shooting and killing crocs all along the river, Sweetheart was always left to enjoy a quiet, peaceful existence.

"We never had no trouble from that big 'gator, we always knew he was there watching us when we went to get turtle or barra, but he never go for us, not even for our dogs and we never try to shoot or spear him. I saw that big croc a lot of times but he just sat there looking at me, he never tried to get me or my dugout. I shot a lot of big crocs but we always left Old Man Sweets Lookout alone", said Nugget.

"The reason he started biting and attacking those boats and motors is because of the noise they made on his billabong", he added.

Whatever the reason, this first chapter in the Saga of Sweetheart ends with both crocodile and human beings living in peaceful co-existence. Sweetheart probably enjoyed the peace and tranquility of his section of the Finniss River for some 40 to 50 years gradually increasing in length and girth, gathering a harem of lady friends about him, sireing hundreds of saurian offspring and occassionally rising to challenge and defeat a rival for supremacy of the billabong..Life for Sweetheart was good, the years rolled by, the food was plentiful, he was king of the river and he grew fat, outwardly it was a lazy life. But all that was soon to change, the truce, the "NGIRRWAT" between man and crocodile was about to be broken.

The fascinating saga of Sweetheart had begun, his period of notoriety was underway, soon his name would be a household word throughout Australia and much of the world.

N.T. native with a young croc captured - State Reference Library

Chapter 2

THE SHOOTING STARTS

Max Sargent & Ray Petherick

It was the year 1924 when well known Territory bushman and identity Max Sargent and his father set up Stapelton Station. It was a massive place, taking in land from the Daly River almost to South-port and including the Finniss River area. I recently caught up with the old bushman who still lives at Ironstone Lagoon in the Finniss area. He picks up the saga.

"Old Charlie Stead was the first professional croc shooter to move into that area in 1934. I never used to shoot professionally - just to protect my stock", he said. "The crocs were really thick all through that country, still are. I counted 107 crocs in one day on the saltwater Finniss. As a matter of fact, I had a pet croc as a kid. He used to go on mustering camp with me in a greenhide cage. He was about 3'6" long. I kept him tied up by the leg to a tree for the first few months but after that he would follow me about just like a dog. I used to feed him mince meat. I had him in the bath tub back at the station but someone took him out to their car and didn't wind the window up and he escaped. I met him again years later face to face while swimming in the creek. I'm sure it was him, he was about 7 foot and we had a staring match right in the middle of the river. Maybe he recognized me as we went our separate ways in peace," he added.

Max told me how in 1956 he corraled a herd of horses in a paddock adjoining the Finniss River, the days were hot and dry and so to escape the heat the horses waded into the cool, shady waters.

"We lost 17 horses in 5 days to those damn crocs" he said. "I don't know how many cattle. Sweetheart wasn't a real big croc. There's one alive down there that is well over 20 feet, still there today, below Lindner's Landing" he said.

I asked Max his theory on why Sweetheart had turned rogue.

"Rogue crocs are made, not born", he said. "Sweetheart was turned from a normal croc into a rogue by people annoying him during the breeding and nesting season."

When I inquired if he knew of any early attacks on boats in the area, he told me the story of the two croc shooters in the early 1950's. Both dropped exhausted into their boat after a hard nights shooting and skinning. One, who still had on his gum boots, had his legs hanging over the side and a croc latched onto one of his boots and managed to tear it completely off the shooter's protruding foot!

Max himself has experienced several personal encounters with the big saurians. For a while he fed several from his boat while engaged in fishing professionally. One time, on the saltwater Finniss, his dog was standing in the doorway of the boat's cabin when a hungry croc raised its head right up over the transom. Upon spying the dog and obviously thinking it would make an easy meal, the big "mud gecko" as they are affectionately known here in the north, lunged at the quivering canine. The attack propelled the croc completely clear of the water, shooting it half way down the deck of the cabin cruiser where it managed to jam its head under a protruding railing.

There stuck tightly against the deck, the big croc tossed and thrashed about, creating enough noise and pandemonium to bring Max on the run, rifle at the ready. With a neatly placed bullet in the brain, one dog hungry croc departed to the happy hunting ground.

E. Hill in the book "The Territory" reports one croc coming up to a station homestead and taking meat hanging in a tree, while next day hearing a commotion in the kitchen raced out to find a 16 foot croc crashing through his pots and pans!

While interviewing these bushmen , aborigines, cattlemen and old croc shooters, one thing impressed me and really caused me to change my mind about crocs and even feel sad for Sweetheart. Almost to a man these fellows felt the croc's reputation as a man-eater was over dramatised. Certainly they all displayed a healthy respect for the big reptiles. Many had been attacked, but in respect to the years and the numbers of crocs that they came in contact with the incidence of attacks were small. Of course they grew up knowing just what precautions to take. Also as strange as it may seem, almost all the fellows who really knew something about crocs, felt Sweetheart was not at fault. Somewhere along the line something like a shooting or being hit and injured by a boat or motor had turned Sweetheart from a normal crocodile into a rampaging, destructive rogue. I could not help but recall Max Sargent's words "Rogue crocs are made not born".

Maybe, just maybe an ex croc shooter by the name of Ray Petherick holds the key to the mystery.

THE 1940's - 60's. RAY PETHERICK

During the 1940's and 50's probably little contact was made between white man and Sweetheart, apart from men like George Barkus and Charlie Stead who had moved into the area to make their living by shooting "gators". Another well-known croc hunter was Ray Petherick who started shooting the Reynolds and Finniss River areas in 1949 and carried on right up until the last day - 30 June 1971 - the day open slather croc shooting was banned forever.

Ray was part of the immediate post-war migration to the North. He was one of the few to develop a close rapport with the wild environment and is acknowledged as a superb, sensitive naturalist and field expert of swamp living crocodiles - second to none.

I caught up with Ray at his camp at Petherick's Rain Forest, a lovely green oasis not far from the Finniss River where he has spent much of his life. Ray picks up the story himself.

"I shot a lot of crocs, including plenty of big ones in Sweets Lookout in the 1950's. It was a good area for big crocs and there are still a lot there too, particularly that hole. Lots of crocs in the 16 to 17 foot range. Nugget, George and Charlie used to shoot there and the aborigines from the station used to hunt turtles along the banks. Generally speaking, we never had much trouble with big crocs. All the years I hunted them I was only attacked a few times. Not many. There have been a few crocs leave their billabongs and get around behind me, stalking me but I always carried a rifle to protect myself. My wife's sister was taken by a croc, down on the Daly River but that was a long time ago, back in the 1930's."

I asked Ray if the account I had heard of him being the first to have a "run-in" with Sweetheart was true. Did he hold the distinction of being the first human to feel the wrath of Sweetheart? This was his reply.

Hauling in a harpooned alligator, Wildman

E. JACKO -86-

"I did have a narrow escape with a big croc in Sweets Lookout in 1958. It was about a 16 to 17 footer but I don't know if it was Sweetheart or not - he wasn't a celebrity then. It was a dark night about 9 pm. I was out on the water paddling past a little creek that runs off the main waterhole. Out of the corner of my eye I happened to notice a croc and so I landed the dinghy and sneaked overland toward where it lay. The torch was a bit flat and so I couldn't see the croc properly. He was a big fellow about 16 feet, I would say, and just lying on a buffalo pad, right where the buffs cross the little creek. As I approached he submerged in the shallow water and then suddenly with a huge splash he leapt right out of the water at me. The bank was about 2 foot high but in a huge mountain of spray he landed right on top of the bank and tried to knock me backwards into the water. Fortunately for me there were just too many palm trees for him to get at me clearly. I whipped up my rifle and fired at him and he rolled back into the creek. I think I hit him as he writhed around splashing water and foam everywhere. Remember it was 9 pm and pitch dark so all I could really make out was the reflection off the water on the horns on his back. It all happened so quickly, I mean, one minute he was in the water and the next he was 6 feet away from me on the bank trying to have a go at me" said Ray.

"If I had been standing on a clear bank he would have knocked me into the water for sure".

The hunter had become the hunted!

"Then the croc came up again. He scuttled up the bank and tried to run overland to get back to the main waterhole. Racing through the jungle the big fellow managed to get himself tangled in a whole lot of Pandanus and so I fired a second shot from my .303. Again I think I hit him, this time in the back. As I fired, the Pandanas broke and he rolled into the waterhole and disappeared beneath the water. We went out looking for him but he never surfaced. We waited for a while and then paddled back to the bank where I got out leaving Johnny Faulkner still in the dinghy. While I was away the croc surfaced again and charged headlong at our dinghy. Johnny started yelling at the croc as it attacked - he was still in the boat - and then it went down again."

Had Sweetheart launched his first attack on a boat?

"We never saw him again", continued Ray. "We waited around for 3 days but couldn't see the croc. He could have gone under the floating grass and died. We just don't know. Dead crocs always float to the top after 3 - 4 days" said Ray.

I feel that the croc was probably Sweetheart because it was the right size, in the right place (Sweets Lookout), it was the first time a boat had been attacked and after Sweetheart's death no more attacks on boats were made and when Sweetheart was finally captured and stuffed, his skeleton revealed two possible bullet wounds.

One bullet was still lodged in the spine. These may have been the bullets fired by Ray Petherick in this encounter.

"I have never known a croc to attack a boat before, at least in the areas I used to shoot", said Ray.

I put the question to him of why Sweetheart became a rogue. What had made him attack boats and motors?

"I don't know, unless he had been wounded in the ear or something. The noise of motors might have irritated or affected his hearing. I don't know. I have been attacked in the Reynolds River during the daytime but I think he was going for me, not the canoe. Crocs are territorial and don't usually let other big males into their areas. This big one was living under a mat of floating grass off a side creek. Another big one has taken its place now. I doubt though if a croc would mistake a boat for another croc (boats and motors make too much noise). It might, if they were starting to mate - they start to mate around September. I suppose a boat could look like another big croc trying to move in", he finished.

So ends the first encounter involving violence. Was it Sweetheart? Was it the start of the rogue crocodile's long and terrifying saga or was it just a coincidence?

E.JACKO -86-

E. Jacko -86-

E. Jacko -86

Chapter 3

STATION LIFE

Clyde Reborse

The Finniss River is a beautiful spot, lying approximately 40 miles south west of Darwin, as the crow flies. Its broad expanses of river meander through paper bark swamps and lush floodplains that support a wide variety of wildlife, until it finally ends up on lovely sandy beaches where the river enters the Arafura Sea. The station is picturesque especially the homestead site which is located overlooking a 20 mile long, permanently lush, green, fertile floodplain. In the background the Finniss River itself wanders along, its cool deep waters are home to turtles, barramundi and of course crocodiles. The Finniss area has always been a known haunt for these saurians and famous especially for big specimens like Sweetheart.

While researching material for this book, I discovered recorded accounts of crocodile attacks as far back as the early 1900's.

It was the Reborse brothers who immigrated to these wild lands from Utah, USA and established the Finniss River Cattle Company back in the late 1950's. Lee and Clyde arrived here and set up the station with their families. Clyde still lives in Darwin today, a rough, tough, no-nonsense cowboy - a man of few words. Like Max Sargent, Clyde probably knows the Finniss River area well, having ridden on horseback over every square inch of it many times.

Clyde certainly had his own experiences to add to the intriguing Sweetheart saga. During my interview with him I enquired about how bad the crocs were during his time on the river and if he had had any first-hand encounters.

"I came up on a big fellow one time while I was on horseback", he said. "He had just bit a cow and broke her hip and had her down in the water. I'd say it was probably Sweetheart or whatever you guys call it. I'd say that big croc would have run that whole section of the river. But it's only my supposition, I don't know. This was during the Wet Season in a channel that runs into Lindner's Landing. I used to ride the river to check the fences and I came up onto this hell of a big croc, he had this cow down, but she wasn't dead. He was a real big croc, 16 to 18 feet I'd guess. He had just bit her and broke her hip, the whole left side of her body was crushed. The cow was lying in water

about 3 feet deep, just head up and out of the water. When he caught sight of me he just took off, shot out into the middle of the channel and just lay there looking at me. I knew the old cow was a goner and if I had a rifle with me I would have shot her as well as the croc. There was nothing I could do and so I rode on to check the fences. When I came back several hours later the cow was gone. Apparently he had taken her, dragged her down beneath the water.

I saw a horse taken one time too, back in the mid 60's. A big croc bit it in the same place, took the horse's guts right out. It was one of those things you only get to see once in a lifetime. After the attack the horse just bolted off into the scrub, dragging its guts along behind it. When it reached the road it just fell over dead. We used to call the horse Billy the Kid.

Don't tell me there's no crocs about, there were miles of them along that river", he said.

E. Hill in the book "The Territory" writes of crocs in 1908:

"Gore at Marrakai killed 42. At Katherine crossing they were taking drovers horses."

The writer reported one station owner on the Daly River losing eleven horses and another fourteen, all to crocs.

I asked Clyde if they used to have trouble with the crocs coming up around the station itself - the homestead being close to the river.

"We were down mustering one day, Larry Bright and me, at the beginning of the Wet Season," Clyde continued. "There was a patch of cane grass right out in front of the house, well there was a big croc lying right there. I remember it well. The plains were just starting to flood, we rode around the corner and there was a second big one. I have seen four to six of those big crocs in a mob. They ate all our horses. I don't know how many horses we lost to crocs, maybe fifteen or twenty head! The number of cows that got eaten is anybody's guess. We never did have any people taken but it was just luck that they weren't.

The first I knew about Sweetheart, if it was Sweetheart, was from the aboriginal women. They used to go over to Sweets Lookout billabong hunting and fishing. That big croc was often watching

33

Yes, they knew he was there alright. This would probably be in the late 60's or early 1970's, I think. The native women wouldn't go over there anymore because they saw this giant croc and while they didn't actually have any trouble with him, they knew what a big croc is capable of doing" he laughed.

Few people ever actually saw Sweetheart, even many of the attack victims never actually saw the croc, obviously most would have had one thing on their mind - survival! So I asked Clyde if he ever laid eyes on Sweetheart for sure.

"Well", he said. "I saw a croc the size of Sweetheart many times, I dunno if it were Sweetheart or not", he laughed.

"That big croc they call Sweetheart, he lived there alright. I came along there one day in my Toyota, he was just lying on the bank. He was huge. When he heard me he just slid off the bank and disappeared. That was just below where he turned my boat over."

You must understand that at this stage of the story no one had named or identified Sweetheart, it was just referred to as "the big croc at Sweets Lookout". The name etc was all in the future, yet to happen. But Clyde did know there was one big, aggressive, monster croc in Sweets Lookout who had for some reason taken a distinct dislike to boats and outboard motors. But why the hatred for boats? Clyde offered his ideas on the subject.

"The reason the croc attacked boats was the simple fact that they were in the area they laid their eggs - it was just protecting its family", he said.

But why only some boats, why weren't all boats attacked?

Clyde continued. "Well at the particular time my boat and the safari boat were attacked they were the only boats in the area. I think it was during the breeding season or when the females were hatching their eggs. Boyne Litchfield was attacked twice, Last of the Wild Safaris' boat was hit, Dave Lindner the ranger and three or four other boats were all attacked during this time of the year."

"In September 1978 I was driving to Sweets Lookout when I spied my dinghy turned completely upside down. The boat had been there for two weeks or more and had never been touched. The day before this I noticed a Government helicopter culling buffalo in the area and I thought they had shot a hole through it, at least that was my first reaction when I saw it overturned. But then when I got to the boat and turned it over I noticed a big tooth mark and scrape on the outboard. Sweetheart had attacked. For no reason at all, the crazy croc had got stuck into it! One of his teeth went right into the top of the motor while another scraped the side. Apparently he just couldn't get a decent grip and rolled the whole lot - boat and motor upside down. Both were floating upside down when I just happened along. That's no mean effort to roll a dinghy and outboard motor!" he said

After that Clyde got onto Peter McCauley the Commissioner of Police and said "Look, do something about this croc, it's getting really dangerous."

That's when the fun started - the story really began to warm up.

During Clyde's days on the Finniss, Sweetheart became quite a celebrity world-wide. Film crews from the ABC and the Mike Willesee Show made the rough, dusty journey to this remote isolated billabong trying to shoot some pictures of this gigantic saurian and his personal vendetta with boats. One film crew even came from the good old USA to sight the ugly reptilian, even if their primary reason for being in the Northern Territory was to shoot a film on Barramundi.

Sweetheart had become a celebrity - a film star!

Hunting and fishing trophies 1920's

Boyne and his truck used for hauling croc s▸

Boyne and family inspect a trophy

Chapter 4

SWEETHEART MEANS BUSINESS

Boyn Litchfield

Up until now Sweetheart had not attracted special attention, his confrontations with man and boat being little more than that expected of a large saltwater crocodile. But all that was about to change and change drastically!

It is September, several months before the monsoonal storms roll down from the Orient to engulf Northern Australia in a deluge. The heat is oppressive, the humidity is high and sweat rolls down from the brow of a fisherman. He wipes it away with his sleeve and turns to his companions. "It sure is hot. I just wish it would rain, that would cool things down a bit".

All is quiet, deathly still, save for the occassional rumble of thunder miles away across the northern sky. Suddenly there is a loud crash as something huge strikes the aluminium boat. Panic seizes the party as the dinghy rocks crazily, almost capsizing completely. The scream of tortured metal adds to the terror and then a grotesque snout appears over the boat's stern.

"Crocodile", screams the man. "Crocodile", he yells again for unnecessary emphasis.

The fisherman lurches forward in a desperate attempt to seize the boat's paddle. As he does so the croc again hits the boat sending the man flying over the seats and crashing on his back. The lady hurtles over the side of the tilting boat, catches hold of the seat and holds on for dear life. The croc proceeds to shake the boat much like a terrier shakes a rat.

In desperation now the angler reaches for the small outboard motor, grasps the starter rope and pulls with every ounce of strength. The motor coughs and dies. Again with renewed vigour he hauls on the starter rope again and again. Finally the little engine starts, coughs and misses and then begins to fire. Instantly the crocodile's attention is averted from the boat to the throbbing motor and with an almost frenzied dive Sweetheart seizes onto the propellor succeeding in bending and mangling it. The woman in the boat flashes a look at the fisherman, the moon illuminating the terror and panic on her face. Maybe sixty seconds have transpired

but it seems like an eternity. Again the croc presses the attack on the boat, almost succeeding in hoisting its huge frame up onto the side of the craft, perhaps in a tactical move to capsize the small dinghy. Water pours in over the side swamping the craft. Lightning flashes across the sky adding to the already eerie atmosphere. The enormous, prehistoric looking head of the rogue croc has been burned forever into the minds of the three anglers.

As quickly as the savage attack began, Sweetheart slips beneath the dark murky waters and disappears. In a few seconds it's all over - the materialised reality of this phantom of the night is gone.

Territory born ex-crocodile shooter Boyne Litchfield his son Peter and Dulcie Pattenden were the three night anglers on whom Sweetheart vent his fury. Boyne is the son of famous Top End pioneer and writer Jessie Litchfield ("Grand Old Lady of the Territory"). He probably knows the waters of the Finniss River as well as any white man alive. From the early 1930's right through to the end of the crocodile hunting days, Boyne hunted, shot and skinned literally thousands of these saurians.

He remembers well the large numbers of big crocs along the Finniss River.

While researching material for this book, I came across an article by noted Australian writer, Ernestine Hill, written in 1939 in which she describes Boyne as one of the gamest men alive. She relates a story of when Boyne was just 19 years old and croc shooting professionally on the Adelaide River.

He had shot about a 15 foot croc and it started to sink, so Boyne seized a rope and with a Tarzan dive from the lugger's mast, he hit the water, dived down to the bottom and secured the croc by the tail. That may not sound much but as Hill points out, Boyne had virtually bet his life on that shot. If the croc had only been wounded, he would most likely never have seen daylight again. Such is the man.

This 5m monster was captured in a Top End
  river

Boyne Litchfield setting a croc bait and snare

Damage to Boyne's boat and motor done by
Sweetheart - holes punched through aluminium
and motor cowling cracked

Crocodile hunters in the 60's take a victim

I asked him about the largest croc he had ever seen.

"Twenty and a half feet was the biggest I saw on the Daly River, but the biggest I ever shot was 18'6" on the Finniss".

Boyne related to me a first hand account of a croc attack he had witnessed some years ago.

"Our lugger was anchored off Bathurst Island one evening when I noticed a native dugout paddling our way with two aboriginal men and a woman inside. I was horrified to see the ugly head of a massive croc appear alongside the tiny canoe. That big croc placed both his front paws on the gunnel of the dugout and just tipped it to one side. In a few seconds he snatched the woman into his powerful jaws, disappeared beneath the waters and was gone. There was hardly a scream or a splash - it just all happened so quickly", he said.

Actually it was Boyne that first introduced me to the fishing pleasures of the beautiful Finniss River. At the time I was the proprietor of a fishing and hunting goods store in Darwin. From time to time I pleaded with the station owner, Clyde Reborse to let me come fishing but he was a tough customer and always turned me down. Boyne had always fished these waters and offered to take me so the acquaintance grew. It wasn't long before I realised

Boyne was far from the ordinary average Darwin fisherman.

The Finniss River is a lure fisherman's nightmare - inundated with submerged logs, snares, obstacles and trees. Consequently, as we trolled up and down the river hoping to entice the elusive barramundi from their haunts, we would usually succeed in snagging a few lures. Before I had a chance to say my name, Boyne would strip to his underpants and dive overboard, a few seconds underwater and the old gentleman would break the surface with the missing lure.

I was really concerned about the crocs and on more than one occassion I told him so.

"Ever had any trouble with crocs here?" I queried. "No" was his usual reply. "There are still a few about, but mainly freshies (Johnson River crocodiles), none that would bother you".

It was a reply that never really convinced me or for that matter ever managed to entice me into those dark, murky waters. The lure could stay there as far as I was concerned, there were plenty more back at the shop, that was my philosophy. Had I known the whereabouts and habits of a one "Sweetheart", well suffice to say I would never have even put my hands in the water!

BOYNE'S SECOND ATTACK

Boyne is a remarkable man, a true character of the north, one of those fast disappearing breed that seem larger than life. To him goes the honour of not only being the first man "officially" to feel a "Sweetheart embrace" - he was attacked twice by the giant rogue croc.

The first attack took place on September 14 1975, twelve months later again found him back at Sweets Lookout fishing. This time he had invited a British school teacher, Brian Jones to try his luck for the fabled barramundi. The two were enjoying a good days fishing, trolling nonchalantly along in the balmy heat of early evening. Suddenly the boat jerked to a halt, the motor coughing with an abrupt seizure. Boyne picks up the story again.

"I thought we had hit a submerged log, as is often the case on these jungle rivers. I stood up and leaned over to clear whatever was fouling the prop, when suddenly Sweetheart lunged again and seized the motor in its mouth, shaking it so violently that it bit a piece clean out of the cowling. It just cracked like eggshell! The force exerted by those jaws was just incredible. In fact, the attack was so ferocious as it shook the motor that it knocked both Brian and myself flying off our feet."

After a few seconds Sweetheart released its prey, swam some distance away, turned and charged the boat again. This time it struck the aluminium hull with its massive teeth, popping the thin metal skin in four places as if it had been a soft drink can. Again the croc broke off its attack and vanished into the night, leaving the two men in the half submerged dinghy with four gaping holes, a wrecked outboard and some very shattered nerves and still some 1 to 1.5 kilometres from their campsite.

This had been the most savage attack to date.

Being the bushman that he is, Boyne hit on an idea to enable them to limp back to base.

"We paddled the dinghy ashore, pulled it up on to the bank and emptied out the water", he said. "Then we proceeded to repair the damage Sweetheart had made in the boat with its teeth. We used strips of paperbark, rolled tightly together and jammed into the holes. Once the bark hit the water it began to swell and plug the leak. We were able to paddle back to camp, although it seemed to take forever and naturally we were wary of the big toothed gecko! We were both shaken by the ordeal, the ferocity of this attack was unsettling to say the least, and so that night we slept with camp fires all around us."

Although the two dozed off neither really slept. Sweetheart had begun his rampage of nautical aluminium destruction with a vengence.

I asked Boyne if he had ever seen Sweetheart again since those eventful days.

"Many times", he replied. "I saw Sweetheart dozens of times, both before and after those attacks but we never clashed again. In fact, the day before he first attacked us, he swam up to my boat and even dived right under us, just giving us the once over. Yes, I saw that big fellow many times, especially at night, he was easily recognisable, but we never clashed again", said Boyne, drifting off into a spell of reminising.

"Mind you, I was a lot more cagey after those attacks, and I avoided his lair when I was on the river at night".

I asked Boyne what in his experienced opinion was the reason behind Sweetheart turning bad.

"I believe the croc was simply defending its lair, its territory, its lady friends from what he mistook for a rival. The attacks usually took place during the breeding season. I certainly don't think there was any real intention of taking people. He had plenty of chances if he had wanted to do that. On the first day we were attacked all three of us had been swimming and no more than 100 yards from where he later attacked the boat.

When he knocked those two fellows into the river, he could easily have taken them if that was his intention. No, I think it was a purely territorial thing to drive rivals away. That sort of thing is common with crocs you know", he said.

"It seemed the motor was what really got him all stirred up. There appeared to be some bad association with the motor."

Things were really hotting up now. Sweetheart had more or less issued his own ultimatum. Any boat or motor daring to invade the privacy of his lair was considered fair game and would pay the appropriate penalty for the audacity of daring to do so. Certainly boats would be the subject of his close scrutiny and attention at all times.

As any victim will tell you, once you have experienced a "Sweetheart embrace", it is an experience that remains with you for the rest of your life!

Chapter 5

"NEVER SMILE AT A CROCODILE"

Ken Phillips

It was a hot steamy day in mid November 1976, Police Officer Ken Phillips, his two young sons Michael (6), Matthew (9) and friend Merv Alchin had decided to try their luck for barra at Sweets Lookout on the Finniss River.

The journey from Darwin had been hot, dusty and tiring and so they arrived around 10 am anxious to get into the water and shake off the lethargy of the long trip. The barramundi is the magic fish of the north and the locals are willing to travel long distances and suffer prolonged discomforts for the sole pleasure of catching "a big one".

Ken was aware of rumours and the notoriety of a giant croc in the area, in fact he had actually sighted the big saurian on several occassions as it surfaced alongside his boat to give him "the once over".

Like most misadventures not experienced first hand, attacks were something that happened to others. The group settled into the boat, the two young boys seated in the centre. Ken kicked the motor over and they were off into the magic world of the tropical northern river. As they quietly cruised along, fishing rods out, lures occilating crazily through the water, the boys broke into a verse of the song 'Never Smile At A Crocodile' from the musical 'Peter Pan'. Maybe, just maybe, it was an omen of things to come.

It was one of those hot mornings when everyone was half asleep, oblivious to everything around them, the 15 hp Mariner purring contently along, pushing the 3.5 Savage Kestrel quietly through the deep, cool jungle waterway.

Suddenly the boat faltered exactly like so many of the boats that had been attacked previously. Ken looked nonchalantly behind him, thinking the boat had struck a submerged log or snag. Sweetheart struck again, hitting the aluminium boat below the rear seat.

"We didn't see a thing, no croc, nothing", said Ken "But obviously it had homed in on us from the middle of the river - the boat being 20 feet from the bank".

"We were just dumbfounded, unsure of what had

actually happened to us, when suddenly the big croc zoomed right in on us again but this time from underneath. He started to lift the boat right out of the water!"

Indeed Sweetheart had attempted to tip the boat over, in fact as the dinghy dropped back into the water the croc did succeed in laying it right over on its side, causing water to pour aboard.

"In the midst of all this activity Michael was almost thrown out of the boat. Luckily Merv managed to grab a hold of his arm and haul him back into the dinghy!" said Ken.

By now Ken himself had his hands full as he desperately struggled with the motor, grasping and reefing at the starter rope in a frenzied attempt to get the boat moving and away from danger. Sweetheart, still positioned beneath the boat attacked again, this time with such force and ferocity that he lifted the whole outfit clear of the water, spun it around some 180 degrees and sent it crashing back down again but facing completely in the opposite direction!

The little boat jerked and rocked under the severity of the assault. As the occupants fought to regain their balance they were confronted by the massive, menacing head of Sweetheart as he surfaced immediately alongside.

"The croc lifted his head right out of the water, he was there right alongside of the boat, he was close enough for me to have reached out and touched him," said Ken.

"He was huge! We realised immediately that it was Sweetheart, the giant rogue croc, we also realised that we were in trouble, to say the least. He just sat there staring at us, it was scary I tell you. I guess we were still in shock from the first attack" he continued.

By now Ken realised he had fishing line tangled all around his neck.

"How that came about I still don't know, but it was there, probably happened during the time Sweetheart was playing volleyball with us" he said.

"Damn crocodile lifted the whole boat right around so we were facing the opposite direction. Man that beast must have had some strength. I wonder what a 12 foot boat, 15 hp motor, two men and two kids weigh."

Merv sized up the situation quickly, glancing down at the seat in front he noticed Ken's .357 magnum revolver lying in its holster. In a split second he dived for the handgun, desperately trying to prise the weapon from its protective sheath. Meanwhile Ken sat staring at Sweetheart, sort of mesmerised. In a moment of sheer frustration he scooped up his fishing rod and pointed it at the armoured head mere feet away.

"I honestly don't know why I did that, it served no purpose whatsoever. I guess I was pointing to Merv where to shoot," said Ken.

Meanwhile Merv had finally succeeded in wrenching Ken's six shooter free, only to bring it to bear on a patch of bubbles where Sweetheart had submerged and disappeared.

"That croc led a charmed life" said Ken. "But we would have been in more trouble if we had shot and only wounded it, he probably would have come for us with a vengence."

"The kids were terrified, in fact it took me a full year before I could coax young Michael back into the boat."

"I finally managed to restart the motor and we eased forward real slowly. I didn't want to take a chance on antagonising that great big brute again. We were really packing it, I tell you. He really hit that boat something fierce. Later I found he had actually broken off a tooth during the first attack. It was still embedded in the bottom of the boat!"

That was the last the party saw of the marauding croc.

"That was the last I wanted to see of the damn thing" Ken finished. "We just packed up and limped back to camp."

I quizzed him as to his views of the cause of the concentration of attacks on boats by this giant rogue croc.

"I think he must have been shot previously", he said. "I guess he associated the noise of the motor with the pain he suffered from the shooting or the injury received at the time. If that is the case he would be prone to attack any boat and motor he came in contact with. I remember an old croc shooter named Fritz Roemer used to say that crocs never attack on direct instinct, so if that's true, there had to be some reason for hitting all those boats."

Whatever the reason one thing is for sure, the Phillips family will remember the day they encountered Sweetheart for the rest of their lives. And certainly, most certainly, every time they hear the tune 'Never Smile At A Crocodile'.

PERIODICALS SEC
DARWIN COMMUNITY
COLLEGE L.R.C.

BURRELL'S BRAKE
SERVICES
PH. 81 4458

The News
NORTHERN TERRITORY

COUNTRY AND INTERSTATE 25c

AUTO
TRANSMIS
SPECIAL
Adjustments,
Overhauls, Exchar
Ph. 81 8715—81 9
GOYDER ROAD

VOL. 27, NO. 155·   Registered for posting as a newspaper—Category "A"   DARWIN, MONDAY, SEPTEMBER 18, 1978   Telephone 81 6582, 28 Mitchell St .   Darwin. Price 2

Giant crocodile scare:
TWO BOATS SUNK!

By DAVID TROUNCE

TWO Territory Parks and Wildlife Commission officers will act as bait to catch a large saltwater crocodile terrorising fishermen on the Finnis River.

They will try to reconstruct the conditions under which fishermen in small dinghies were attacked in two separate incidents at Sweet's Lookout, 80 kms south-east of Darwin.

The 20-ft croc locked its jaws around one boat, puncturing the aluminium dinghy in six places with its teeth, holding tight for several minutes.

The fishermen, Mr Max Curtis and Mr Ian Watson of Mandorah, broke an esky in half to bail frantically as they motored to shore.

The boat sank as they jumped ashore.

In the second incident on Friday night, Mr Brian Cowen and Mr George Tsakaris, swam 30 metres to shore after the croc struck from underneath and swamped the tiny dinghy.

HUNTERS

The next day when the boat was salvaged, the outboard motor was bitten in half and the fuel tank missing, believed swallowed.

Both aluminium dinghies were owned by tour operators, Last of the Wild Safaris.

Last of the Wild operators, Mr Mal Thomas and Mr Bill Tye, both experienced crocodile hunters, will accompany the wildlife officers on the hunt.

A senior commission officer said today: "We will have to duplicate the conditions and arouse the croc.

URGENCY

"We believe it is probably attacking under territorial instincts, not predatorial," he said.

"We've investigated these reports and decided to take this action as a matter of some urgency.

"But we are treating it as an isolated incident, not a frequent problem.

"Our first option is to see if the croc will come out and repeat it--lf.

'WE WILL BE THE BAIT'

"If it does, we'll attempt to shoot it and retrieve the croc," the spokesman said.

Mr Curtis said that when the croc hit from underneath, it "sounded like when two cars collide."

TEETH

"We held on to the boat like hell, because every time the croc shook, the whole boat shook.

"The teeth came through the bottom, leaving holes the size of my thumb.

"Its mouth open was like looking down the front of a front-end loader," Mr Curtis said.

A third sighting of a crocodile was reported at the weekend when a crocodile was seen off Casuarina Beach, near the Rapid Creek River.

Swimmers quickly left the water, but no attacks were made.

Soviet spies 'in ASIO'

CANBERRA.—A book by a former private secretary to Gough Whitlam claims that the KGB — the Russian secret police — was reported to have infiltrated ASIO, Australia's Security Intelligence Organisation, in 1975.

And according to the author, Richard Hall, the fate of the Soviet infiltrators has been an extraordinarily well-kept secret.

The book also claims that Queensland Premier Joh Bjelke Petersen pressured the Prime Minister, Mr Fraser into deporting a number of Chilean exiles living in Australia, citing security reasons.

He also claims

INSIDE

- 'Sold out to the Bartons': P2.
- NLC chairman given bond: P2.
- Church supports lands right: P4.
- Trace history of your name: P7.
- Plus specials motoring feature.

Iran 'quake toll rising

(TEHERAN),—The   Iranian   east of Iran last night.   suffered serious damage.
One   The quake measured 7.7 on the

YOU'LL never guess who the devil-may-care fellow is hanging for dear life at the back of the speeding motorcycle sidecar unit.

YOU'L
NEVE

Chapter 6

EYEBALL TO EYEBALL

Max Curtain & Ian Watson

Despite the number of attacks taking place on the Finniss, few people were reporting them to the authorities or media. In many cases, as this next story will demonstrate, the reason was fear - fear of criticism, fear of ridicule.

One factor about the whole Saga amazed me and that is that such a series of events, attacks, boat holings, sinkings and capsizing could go on over such a long period of time without the complete story coming forward. In fact, as strange as it may seem, it wasn't until 1985 while Greg Biddell and myself were engaged in research of the events in detail that the whole picture came together. Many of the accounts had never been reported or even discussed - in fact, we aren't 100% sure even now that we have not missed out on encounters and attacks that may have taken place. Perhaps some will remain undocumented forever.

Ex Wildlife Ranger, Dave Lindner had compiled the only detailed and accurate account in existence but our investigations uncovered much even he didn't know about. Several of the attack victims were reluctant to speak up, claiming they had never discussed the subject with anyone, others stated that when they had been interviewed by the media their stories were incorrectly reported, as in the case of one fellow who said, "I was made to look like a galah. Something I said by way of a joke was later shown on a television report as a serious comment."

Certainly a mistrust of the media was something we had to overcome.

During the year 1978, Sweetheart was a busy boy as he continued to wreak havoc on boats. One such encounter would prove to be the longest actual contact between crocodile and man of the entire Saga.

Max Curtain (publican of the Mandorah Inn at the time, now resident in Victoria) and his manager Ian Watson had decided to try their luck with the unpredictable barramundi. Despite patchy rumours and reports of "Croc attacks" and a "rogue croc", the lure of the fish rich Finniss was strong and hard to resist. And so bright and early one hot morning in September the two businessmen were found plying the beautiful waterways of the Finniss River. Ian sat in the stern of the small 3.5 metre boat manning the motor as well as working his

lure in a strong bid to be the first to take a fish. And succeed he did with the first three fish while Max sat in the bow whinging to himself.

"That's three fish now Watson. What the hell are you doing right that I'm not?" Max bellowed to his mate above the noise of the revving outboard motor.

Crash! A sound of impact on metal changed the focus of attention as the boat lurched crazily as though struck by some giant fist. A huge armoured snout shot over the gunnel of the dinghy as two cold beady eyes fastened on Max.

"What the hell's happening - what's that?" he screamed pointing at the massive head protruding at least a foot above the side of the boat.

"Croc!" yelled Ian. "It's a croc."

The massive mouth latched onto the side of the boat and proceeded to shake it so violently that the two men were seemingly powerless to retrieve control from their attacker. They experienced the sensation common to most of Sweetheart's victims of, in the absence of a miracle, being doomed. They were certainly in serious trouble.

When an attack was launched by Sweetheart - he called the shots. In fact Sweetheart was so zealous in the initial attack that he managed to puncture the boat in three places. Teeth popped metal. A hideous screeching, scraping or scouring noise could be heard even above the still revving motor as the croc continued to shake and flay the small boat in a curtain of spray and foam. At one stage the boat tipped to a crazy 30 degree angle with the croc pushing it sideways through the water.

"He must have come straight up from the bottom" said Max. "We never saw anything, we were just quietly cruising the river when 'zonk' and we were hit like a ton of bricks. "This was precisely the method of attack used in at least four other incidents. He shot his ugly snout about 12 to 14 inches clear over the side of the boat, popped his fangs right through the bottom and just hung on for grim death", continued Max.

"Only missed Ian's hand by a couple of inches! He just sat there and shook our boat until he ran out of steam. There was nothing we could do about it - it was his show. Boy, I mean here was this dirty great croc with its head over the side of our boat, directly between me and Ian. I tell you we were packing them!" he continued.

"He must have hung onto our boat for ages - it seemed like forever. (It was probably the longest attack by Sweetheart on a boat). I was only about three feet from its head and we just sat there eyeball to eyeball throughout the whole proceedings. I would have liked to know what he was thinking. He wouldn't have had much trouble with knowing what my thoughts were......my face would have portrayed it all. I remember looking right down its gullett; it was massive and a brilliant orange I kept hoping that it would cut its mouth on the side of the metal boat. I tell you I had a great view right down Sweetheart's throat - we certainly had plenty of time to get well acquainted."

"The outboard motor was roaring its head off the whole time. We left it going as we didn't know what else to do, plus we were so damned scared that neither of us could have moved. After what seemed ages he seemed to run out of steam and so gave us one more shake, just for good measure, then released his grip on the boat, slipped under the water and was gone. That was the last we saw of him, mind you, it was the last we wanted to see of him too!!! We were both pretty scared. You try spending a quarter of an hour eyeballing with the business end of the biggest croc you've ever seen and see how you feel about it. I guess it was the sheer closeness of its huge head that really unnerved me. The eyes were about fourteen inches apart", he finished.

As suddenly as it had started it was all over. Max and Ian sat staring at the spot where the huge croc had disappeared. The boat gradually began to fill with water through the holes Sweetheart's ample teeth had made.

"We ripped a foam esky in half in nothing flat so we could both bail the boat at the same time - I mean we were shipping water real smartly and we both had one thought in mind and that was to get to hell out of there! Some distance away we spotted two fishermen in a boat. They had apparently witnessed the whole attack and so we headed straight for them. We were going to get out of our fast submerging craft and join them. The only problem was that when we got to within about ten feet of them they started yelling at us to go away or get another boat or something. It turned out that their boat was smaller than ours and just wouldn't take the four of us. We started yelling back to them to get out of the place - the croc was still about and he was madder than a hornet. Their little boat wouldn't have stood much of a chance if attacked. As a matter of fact, I wondered what the two guys were playing at, just sitting there not trying to move. It turned out later that they were in such a panic to start their motor and get away that they ripped the starter rope clean out! The two

CROCODIL WARNIN

They are on the attack

By FRED McCUE

CROCODILE attacks on boats in Territory rivers could become more prevalent in the next few years.

The reptile which has so far eluded all attempts to capture him, has been involved in dozens of attacks in the rivers Sweetmans Lookout area.

Wildlife rangers who have been observing the activities of a six-metre crocodile at the Finniss River believes his attacks on dinghys could be a sample of things to come.

The crocodile's latest attack involved a Territory Park's and Wildlife dinghy.

The rangers in the boat were led by local crocodile expert Dave Linder. They were studying the reptile at the time.

The rangers had not sighted the huge saltwater crocodile and were preparing to abandon their search when he loomed out of the murky waters of the Finniss has entered his area of the river.

A wildlife spokesman said the sound of a slowly idling engine is similar to that of a challenging bellow of another crocodile.

It is believed the Finniss River giant is one of the few old reptiles in the Territory which was not hunted by men in outboard boats prior to the animals becoming protected.

Crocodiles which have had this experience show a fear of outboards as they associate the engine noise with the pain of a hunters bullet.

Crocs fatal fascination of motors led this 3.5 metre saltie to attack a coastal barge's propeller. Head is mutilated

just sat there. After what they had just seen they were too scared to even put their hands in the water and paddle. Not that I blamed them either".

The two managed to limp back to camp just as they were about to sink. Max jumped out, tipping the boat over as he did so. Ian scuttled ashore and stood shaking on the bank. They were just setting out in a borrowed boat when they heard a gunshot from downriver.

"Naturally we thought the two guys in the little boat had been attacked and consequently neither of us were too keen to go back but the thought of them in that tiny boat without a motor was a bit much and so off we went", said Max.

"We arrived on the scene to find that they hadn't seen the croc but had just fired off a shot to let us know they were still waiting. We hooked them up and towed them back to camp".

"Ian and I decided not to say anything to anybody about the whole deal. We thought that it sounded too much like a cheap publicity stunt to be believed and so we planned just to shut up and say nothing. I mean, really, it sounded like another Loch Ness Monster job. Hell, we needed publicity like that like we needed a hole in the head. Remember, we didn't know about all these other attacks that were taking place. I mean if it had have been a tiger or something well, I wouldn't

mind being saddled with a nickname like "Old Tiger" but I ask you, who would want to answer to a nickname like "Old Croc"? As a matter of fact when a reporter from the Mike Willesee Show came to see me I denied knowing anything about the whole thing, denied it was even me. He said to me, 'Come on now Mr Curtin, I have an eye witness to the attack' so I finally sat down and told them the whole story."

Max went on to tell me that apart from that reporter I was the only person he had spoken to about the attack in any length. It's unfortunate that some of the media do tend to exaggerate or "colour" stories, sensationalize is a better word, I guess. Truth is stranger than fiction anytime.

These reports were mild however compared to some of the overseas reports that had Sweetheart eating everything from outboard motor tanks to even the actual outboard motor itself!

Max and Ian signed the safari camp's guest book that day - "14/9/78 Curtin and Watson. Armour plated boats only. Too close for me, but what an experience, who will believe us?"

It was a caption that had a final touch of irony as on arrival back at the Mandorah Hotel the two victims were greeted by Ian's unbelieving wife as they related the story of the attack.

"Don't pull my leg", she said. "It's just another excuse for you two to get on the booze!"

Chapter 7

A NARROW ESCAPE

Brian Cowan

Brian Cowan and George Tsakissiris are both long time Territory residents and both keen fishermen. As with the other "victims" before them, it was this latter interest that would bring them into contact with Sweetheart.

On the 15th September 1978, the two friends were winging their way towards the Finniss River in a light aircraft, intent on doing a spot of night barra fishing. Upon their arrival at the bush strip at the Finniss Station they were met by "The Last of the Wild Safari's" guide Max Davidson and then driven to the Sweets Lookout area.

"George and I had been doing a bit of night fishing at other places and so we wanted to try for some barra down on the Finniss" said Brian.

"So away we went, as it was, there had been an attack on another boat the night before we arrived. We actually saw the boat, it had a couple of nice holes in it. I remember telling Max that we weren't going anywhere near where that happened. However once you get out on the river it's hard to know where you are, so I don't know if we did end up near the spot or further downriver. Anyway we were enjoying the fishing - it was a beautiful moon-lit night and we had hooked about ten good barra - we landed five and lost five. Some of the fish were slipping off the hooks, so we pulled up and were changing to bigger lures. It was dark, I guess it would have been around 8 o'clock at night. We mucked around a bit getting set up, then I started the motor. As soon as it kicked over there was a hell of a whack that sent me flying off the back of the seat into the middle of the boat. It scared hell out of me I tell you. George was sitting in the bow and he nearly fell overboard into the water, luckily he managed to grab a hold of something and stop himself.

However in doing so he almost tipped the boat over. We actually tipped right up on the side and the boat started filling with water, almost right up to the gunnels. It wasn't quite to the top, but it was enough, we were going straight down. Fortunately for us the wind was blowing in the right direction and we were drifting toward the bank on the right side where we had left the vehicles. If it had been the other side of the river we would have been in big trouble, there's a lot of crocs on that side as we found out next day", said Brian.

Apparently what had happened was Sweetheart had been lying on the bank as the two fishermen passed quietly by. Slipping into the water, the big croc had stealthily approached the boat unnoticed as they changed their lures. Then at precisely the moment Brian had started the motor, the rogue croc struck and struck with a vengence. The attack was so powerful that it almost succeeded in capsizing the dinghy, knocking both occupants sprawling and sending an expensive shotgun, four fishing rods and assorted tackle to the bottom of the muddy lagoon.

"He hit the boat right underneath where I was sitting, right under my backside. We took some photos of the damage and you can see just where he hit. Looks like he came straight up from the bottom. How he did it beats me, he never actually punctured the metal, it was a much stronger boat than the one that was holed. However there were teeth and scratch marks all over the bottom" said Brian.

At this stage only seconds had elapsed but the two fishermen knew they had been in a battle, and so they decided to do the only thing they could do - dive overboard and swim for safety.

"We just bolted", said Brian.

"We woke up straight away as to what it was and took off. George hit the water first, but started swimming in a circle - I just couldn't get around him - so in my panic I swam right over the top of him and hit the bank first. I yelled out to him, "Are you with me pal?"
"He had swam into a log and climbed up it to get onto the bank. When he managed to clamber out of the water he was shaking like a leaf."

"I think that b..... touched me while I was swimming!" he blurted out excitedly.

"But I reassured him that it was just me swimming over his back that he had felt".

Meanwhile Sweetheart had broken off the first attack, swum up river and then returned to hit the boat savagely again.

"He grabbed that outboard mate and just shook it to bits, ripped the cowling right off the top and then crushed the side right in", said Brian.

"The motor was ripped around badly".

Meanwhile the two anglers had dragged themselves ashore dripping wet and bare footed.

"As soon as we hit the bank we shot through". said Brian. "But we were barefooted and during the walk back to the campsite I ended up with over thirty Pandanus splinters in my feet. I tell you it was damn painful. Maxie Davidson had to dig them out with a pocket knife", he said.

Following the attack, safari operator Max Davidson quickly organised a second boat and he zoomed off into the night to investigate. When they arrived on the scene, it looked like a major battle had taken place, the dinghy was completely upside down with the fuel tank floating beside it. All the contents of the boat which included rods, tackle and shotgun, were lost and so they wisely decided against staying to check things out in the dark just in case Sweetheart was still in the area and in his ugly mood.

"Next morning we took off at daylight with a few aborigines and went back to the attack site", continued Brian.

On their arrival they were again greeted by the up-turned boat, looking for all the world like some bloated, forlorn dead whale. This time however the motor's fuel tank was nowhere to be seen, probably having sunk. (This would later be reported in a British newspaper as having been swallowed by Sweetheart along with the actual outboard motor!)

"We made up a gaff and started to dredge the bottom for our gear. The shotgun belonged to someone else and I understand it was worth A$1000. I lost two rods and a bucket full of lures. In all, we never recovered, four rods. It was difficult work as the water was fairly deep - fifteen to twenty feet. The boat belonged to the safari people and believe me Sweetheart had given it a real going over".

Brian summed the episode up this way.

"It was an experience of a lifetime, but one I wouldn't like to go through again! I tell you what, I'm still frightened of crocs today, I treat them with the respect they deserve. Funny thing about it all is I still haven't seen Sweetheart to this very day. I have seen a photo of him that's all. I guess I'll get to the museum one day and have a look".

And the message George and Brian left in the safari operators guest book?

"Thanks Max. We loved our swim at midnight but not our partner".

The motor attacked - note the section bitten out of the cowling - Photo courtesy Max Davidson

INCHES from injury . . . the arrow, at right, shows just how close the FinnissRiver crocodile's teeth came to injuring a fisherman sitting in the attacked aluminium dinghy.

Croc missed by inches

Mandorah inn manager, Mr Ian Watson, was sitting on the seat when the croc's teeth pierced through the aluminium like a tin-opener.

He believes that if the croc had struck anywhere else on the boat apart from the strengthened seat structure, it would have ripped the side off.

The boat was one of two attacked by a large salt water croc, estimated at between six and seven metres.

The boat was brought back to Darwin by Last of the Wild Safari operators so that officers from the Territory Parks and Wildlife Commission could determine the jaw size of the croc.

Another dinghy was attacked by the same crocodile at Sweet's Lookout, 80km southwest of Darwin, forcing two fishermen to swim to shore when their boat swamped.

Two commission officers, Mr Dave Lindner, and ranger Mr Vic Peterson, went out to the Finniss River area last night to try and catch the crocodile.

They were joined this morning by two crocodile hunters and will attempt to lure the crocodile out and net it.

A spokesman said today if the crocodile proved too big for netting they would have no alternative but to destroy it.

He said they believed the croc was a large male reacting to its territorial instincts during the mating season.

● LAST of the Wild Safari operators, Mal Thomas, left, and Bill Tye, with one of the last of their fishing dinghies. The outboard motor was extensively damaged from the Finniss River crocodile attack last Friday. Last of the Wild have suspended their regular fishing trips on the Finniss until the giant croc is removed or destroyed.

Article courtesy N.T.News - note error. Left is Max Davidson not Mal Thomas

Photo of Sweetheart's teeth damaged and missing
Ian Archibald

Left. Brian Cowan showing spots where Sweet- heart's teeth bit
Photo Max Davidson

Right Top. Tooth hole punched through motor   top

Below. Teeth damage to boat

Right Bottom. Smashed cowling of motor

Photos - D. Lindner

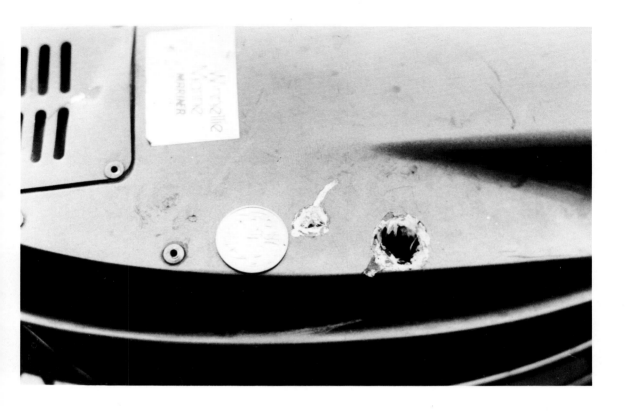

Safari guide Max Davidson (standing)

Chapter 8

THE WHITE HUNTERS

Max Davidson

Max Davidson is a safari guide, having worked around the Top End for years with such outfits as Nimrod, Wimray and The Last of the Wild Safaris, guiding the rich and famous and other hunters and fishermen through the outback. It was to be Max's turn now to enter into the Sweetheart Saga. His first encounter with the old rogue was during the Brian Cowan/George Tsakissiris attack (last chapter.)

"It was my job to take these fellows out barra fishing on the river", said Max. "Despite there having been an attack on Max Curtin the night before, I had never personally encountered Sweetheart. I drove the two boys to the river where we boarded a heavy built dinghy, belonging to Ray Alright of Wimray Safaris, and motored upriver. I wanted to show them the spot the croc had just made an attack. When I did, I told them I didn't want them fishing in that area at all", he said.

With that chore completed Max returned to camp while Brian and George set out for their date with destiny.

"Sometime later I heard a motor coming back down the river, it was old Bill Cunningham. When he got close enough he yelled out to me that there had been another croc attack. I guess I just went white with fright. Without even thinking I jumped into my boat and screamed off back to the landing where I found Brian and George standing, both drenched to the skin and visibly shaken by their ordeal. Fortunately, apart from the ducking and the fright, they were unscathed. Both started jabbering to me their story about the croc, the boat being capsized and the swim they were forced to make. I decided to scoot back and see about the boat and motor, with that Bill Cunningham volunteered to go with me."

"We left the boat upright!" the two called as we roared away from the landing. We arrived on the scene to find the boat completely upside down with the 9.9 hp Mercury outboard under the water with the fuel tank floating alongside. We could see the teeth and scratch marks all over the boat, the motor casing also had bite or chew marks and the cowling was missing altogether. I quickly decided this was no time to play hero and hang around, so we roared off back to pick up my two very wet and very scared clients."

"Back at the base camp I found Brian's feet were so badly cut and lacerated by Pandanus splinters that I had to spend at least a half an hour digging them out with my bush knife!"

That was Max's first encounter with old rogue croc of the Finniss. Some two months later he and partner Stuart McDonald were again on the river with another party of anglers. By now genuine concern had been expressed about the crocodile, even though no lives had been lost. The feeling was that it may only be a matter of time before Sweetheart scored his first victim.

"The rangers had given us permission to shoot Sweetheart", said Max. "But I wasn't that keen on shooting him - he hadn't at that stage harmed anyone and it would be a shame to see a beautiful old animal like that just destroyed. Dave Lindner (the ranger who ultimately captured Sweetheart) didn't want to see him destroyed either; he wanted it captured alive and placed in a crocodile farm. They lent us one of their heavy duty boats, one capable of sustaining a decent croc attack. There were seven of us in that boat, Stuart and I and five anglers from Benalla, Victoria. Again it was just dark and we were upstream about 1½ miles from where the last attack had taken place. It was in a completely different area of the river, we planned to leave that other spot well alone!

We had just caught a barra and were in the process of lifting it into the boat when the boat shuddered as though we had hit a rock or something. The fish swung against my jeans and the hook sunk into my leg. There I was, the fish flapping all over the place, the boat rocking crazily while I'm trying to remove the hook. Stuart had been sitting on the bow of the boat when the croc hit and one of the anglers had to grab him to stop him falling over into the water with the croc. We swung the torch to the rear of the boat and it lit up this hell of a great crocodile. It was Sweetheart without a doubt!

He grabbed a hold and really shook us up badly but the boat was plenty strong enough to stand it. After a few more shakes he seemed to lose interest and swum off. Maybe we weren't as much fun as one of the lighter boats where he could sink his teeth right through the aluminium!" laughed Max.

I asked him for his opinion on crocs, particularly Sweetheart.

"I wouldn't ever get into the water", he said.

"We had a fellow and a girl down here swimming in the river one day. After one of the attacks I took the boat the croc had holed into where this girl worked. I dragged her outside and showed her the holes the teeth had made.

"What's that?" she asked.

"A boat that was attacked by Sweetheart and it happened not more than 100 yards from where you were swimming the other day!" said Max.

"I don't think she has even had a shower since then", laughed Max.

"I like crocodiles and I understand them pretty well, but no one gets me in the water! I have thought about it for years and years and I still can't work out why Sweetheart did what he did. Maybe he felt threatened in some way. They reckon the motor might have sounded like a mating call of another croc, but I don't really think that's it either. He didn't worry about boats and motors most of the time. He obviously wasn't hungry, maybe he was hit, run over or hurt by a boat. It doesn't really make sense. Maybe we all get old and a bit grumpy and cranky.

It was the attack on Clyde Reborses's boat that blows all the theories to pieces. I mean the boat was tied up at the bank and hadn't been used for weeks!

Most of the theories I have heard revolve around the assumption that the motor sounded like another croc, so Sweetheart being territorial, would naturally defend his lair. But that old boat was laying against the bank not even being used.

All of the boats but one were attacked at the stern, around the motor (not true), many of the motors too were hit. I don't know, the whole thing remains a real mystery, one that will probably never be solved now either", he finished.

The pressure to stop Sweetheart was beginning to build rapidly, wildlife officials realised that something had to be done and done quickly to avert a possible death.

And so the stage was set for Sweetheart's ultimate captor, Ranger Dave Lindner, to arrive on the scene. An interesting tussle and battle of wits was about to commence.

The heavy duty boat given by Wildlife Dept.

"Bubba" Tye in the boat Sweetheart attacked

Chapter 9

ANOTHER ONE BITES THE DUST

Carl Blumanis & Dick Gleisnner

The year was now 1979, a fatal year as it would turn out for the giant marauding crocodile of Sweets Lookout. Long time Territorians Dick Gleissner and Carl Blumanis had driven their vehicle down the rough, tough Wangait track through Walkers Ford. Being experienced Top Enders, they knew the Finniss offered some great barra fishing this time of the year and so thought nothing of the long, tough haul to the river.

The two arrived tired, hot and sweaty, the day being particularly oppressive but all that was soon forgotten as the welcome view of the Finniss appeared through the dusty windscreen. They quickly launched the 12 foot Clark boat, kicked over the 25 hp motor and roared off for a date with destiny. Carl picks up the story:

"We were cruising along - it was shortly before lunch I remember", he said. "Everything was quiet and we were both half asleep. It was still a fair way to go to our favourite fishing spot. Suddenly the boat just shuddered as though we had hit a rock or a log but actually we had run right over the top of this massive great croc. I don't know if it was Sweetheart" he continued. "I didn't stick around long enough to ask him. However I did see this hell of a great head rise up out of the water. I mean, the damn thing must have been three foot long (the head that is). In an instant we felt the whole boat just lifted right out of the water. I mean, imagine the strength of that thing, it just hurled the boat out of the water. Dick and I were thrown clear, caterpaulted out into the river while the boat flipped upside down!"

Carl is a little hazy as to what happened over the next few moments, not that one can blame him, one minute cruising along quietly in their boat, the next being shot out into the water by a huge crocodile would probably cause anyone to have a mental blank.

Carl picks up the story again.

"The first thing I remember is starting out for the bank as fast as I could swim. Once I reached it I dragged myself ashore and stood up. The croc was nowhere to be seen but Dick was holding onto the boat. My ticker was really hammering out a beat, I can tell you", continued Dick. "Hell it frightened the life out of me and as soon as I could catch my breath I yelled out to Dick, 'Forget the boat, get to hell out of the water!'

But Dick wasn't leaving the dinghy, by pushing and kicking he managed to maneouvre it to the bank where Carl stood waiting, tree branch in hand to help him out of the water.

"By the time we were able to right the boat we realised we had lost a lot of gear - tackle box, rods and reels including an ABU 9000, lures, tackle etc but worst of all we had lost my beautiful Brno rifle", he said.

It took a while for the impact of the attack to sink into the minds of the two fishermen as they sat down to survey the whole encounter.

"It all happened so fast", said Carl.

"I mean, in seconds the boat was upside down and we were in the water with the meanest, biggest croc I have ever seen in my life. There was no time to think, no time to be scared, everything just happened in a flash. If that croc had wanted us, we were just ready for the picking - there was nothing we could have done about it. Makes me think it must have been asleep or something and we were just unlucky enough to ram him with the boat. I just saw the huge head and the next thing, boom! He tipped the boat upside down and Dick and I were flopping in the water. Could have been the end for us, real easily could have been the end", said Carl thoughtfully.

That was the first and last time the two had sighted what was probably Sweetheart, but it wasn't enough to discourage the two obviously keen fishermen. Dick, being a mechanic, soon had the motor stripped down, cleaned and overhauled ready for action again. And so the two set off down river again, wet, scared and without much tackle...but they still went.

Now that is real dedication!

Some fifteen barra later, the two began to make their way back to the four-wheel drive. However, the story was far from over as darkness had set in by now and they found themselves lost.

The two wandered around in the dark, beaching their boat and staggering along the banks of the river desperately searching for the vehicle. Eventually at 3 am they managed to locate the four-wheel drive but only after jettisoning their entire catch of barramundi.

It's one fishing trip the two will never forget!

Chapter 10

"MAYBE HE JUST DIDN'T LIKE BOATS"

George Haritos

George Haritos is one of Darwin's respected long time residents. A former barramundi and pearl fisherman, the Greek descent, Australian born character is also one of the north's best known croc shooters. I caught up with him at his home in a leafy street in Fannie Bay, a seaside suburb of Darwin.

For many years George hunted and matched his wits against the saurians of these northern waterways, capturing some 4000 of the species, the largest (touching seventeen feet) fell victim to his deadly rifle in the Victoria River.

I spent a pleasant afternoon chatting to the friendly coastal barge skipper as he related his past experiences, thrills, scares, ideas and facts to do with crocodiles. All the time we talked my eyes drifted back to a wire cage, not more than fifty feet from where we sat, which housed George's pet - a ten foot saltwater crocodile!

"Yes sir, crocs are funny things, they have personalities of their own, just like people. Some die quietly when shot, while others go completely crazy. You really never know just what they will do", George said.

"For instance, we had one actually come aboard our fishing vessel out at the Vernon Islands. We had anchored for the night and left some crab bait on deck, so this big old fellow croc came aboard while we were sleeping to get himself a feed! Some are more game than others, I mean it's not unusual for them to try and tip a boat over or to come aboard boats at night."

"One night at Blue Mud Bay we were anchored and I was asleep. One of the native crew came and shook me. 'Come and look at this' he said. We both slipped out onto the deck and there in the half light he pointed out to me the tail of a massive croc lying hard up against the side of the boat. We couldn't see his head but it was obviously waiting for one of us to lean over the side of the boat and then - crunch! Either that or it was waiting to actually come aboard, either way that big fellow meant business", said George.

"What did you do?" I asked.

"I shot him through the head" he replied ever so casually. "You don't mess around with those types. There are many stories of croc attacks etc here in the north", he continued. "Over in the Kimberlies a big croc grabbed a fellow by the foot while he was on a mud bank. Tried to pull him and the boat he was holding onto for dear life into the water".

"I remember a funny story when we were asked to take the Duke of Edinburgh out croc shooting some years back. We went up Pioneer Creek the night before to make sure there were plenty of crocs about. We saw a beauty - about twelve feet - actually we were going to leave him for the Duke to shoot but he started to submerge and the excitement was just too much for me. Anyhow, I let go with this harpoon and in doing so I overbalanced and went overboard after it. I ended up in the water with one very agitated croc. In the excitement and confusion, everybody forgot about me as my brother 'Ningle' fought the croc. Eventually they managed to shoot it after what seemed an eternity to me, and then haul me back on board the boat. It scared the living daylights out of me, I tell you and as I was hauled aboard wet and dripping, this Englishman from the Duke's party took one look at me and said, "I thought it was all part of the act until I saw your eyes!"

George roared with laughter as he recounted the story. It was George who captured the "movie star" crocodile which featured in the film Jedda.

"Actually", said George, "it took the capture of four crocs before the film people were satisfied. Finally they settled for a nine footer captured in the Wildman River."

"I shot a sixteen foot beauty in the Finniss River one time - that's the saltwater Finniss", he said. "It actually attacked our boat. We were in this large pool when we saw this huge croc. At first we thought it was just a log but Roy Edmonds saw it was a croc and fired a shot. It missed and then the gun jammed. The old croc just lay there, so we came alongside and whacked a harpoon into it. Well, the thing just went crazy. It turned around on us attacking the boat repeatedly, tearing large sections of the timber gunnels away. In fact, it

Rohrer.

A Large Alligator Skin.

It measured 18ft 10. The 'gator was caught near Darwin.

punctured the boat, punctured the bottom, pulled fastenings off the transom as he hit us again and again. The harpoon had struck the croc right in the middle of its back but it simply pulled the spear out, swum downriver a bit, turned around and charged right into us. Fortunately, the holes he made were all above the waterline and so we just lightened the boat up to keep from sinking. We managed to beach the vessel and approach the crazed saltie on the mud bank. In fact, we started throwing sticks at him and you better believe he was good and mad. One time he actually leapt about three feet out of the water to bite one of the sticks we had thrown. Caught it right in mid air! Boy, they are fast".

"Eventually I was able to manoeuvre myself into a position to get a shot at him with my shotgun, it hit him in the head and blinded him. But that was far from the end of the fight - that big old fellow just came right up on top of the water defying us. It just seemed he was challenging us or saying 'I just defy you' as he swam straight for us. By now one of the fellows had come up with the 30/06 Garand and drew a bead. But nothing happened, no shot, the safety catch was on. The croc just kept coming straight at us. Eventually we fired and killed it within three feet of where we were standing!"

"That croc was just so big and heavy, it couldn't be carried or even towed. So we just tied it to some mangrove trees and came back later to skin it. Three of us couldn't even turn it over, that's how big it was. It would have weighed about one and a quarter tons", George exclaimed.

"Melville Island used to have some big crocs, one gigantic fellow in particular. Toby Lidy had a fourteen foot dinghy and he came alongside the croc once and it extended beyond both ends of his boat!

The Finniss, the Adelaide, Wildman and Mary River delta systems all had some beauties".

"Do you know how fast some of those crocs are?" quizzed George.

"I once witnessed with my own eyes a duck in full flight scooting over the surface of a river. He was going like a whirlwind, about three feet above the surface of the water. All of a sudden the river just opened up and a sizeable saltwater croc leapt up and seized the duck in mid flight! Took him right out of the sky! And that's no story", he said.

I asked George about some of the top croc shooters of the north.

"Men like Freddie Pocock from the Wildman, Ray Petherick of the Finniss and Tom Vega would be

62

some of the best", he said.

"Crocs are different, just like people. I mean, take that big fellow down on the Finniss. He was mean, real mean. He dressed out around sixty five to sixty six inches across the belly and that's big. He fetched us around $40 and we really earned it. Today that hide would be worth over $1000. Yes sir, that's probably the meanest and toughest croc I have ever encountered. I mean, I've had a few break their teeth off in my boats, but nothing like this fellow in the Finniss".

George was around seventeen or eighteen when he bagged his first croc but it was not until the late 1940's that he took croc shooting up as his chosen profession. The Adelaide, Daly and Wildman Rivers produced prolific numbers of crocs, in fact figures of close to 300,000 have been quoted.

"I saw over thirty crocs in one small stretch of water at Sampan Creek", said George. "Mark my words, they are not stupid", he said. "They will lie in wait for their prey, they bury themselves in the mud, under floating grass or in the lilly pads - just waiting for some unsuspecting animal to come along. They are fast too, very fast.

I have shot them when they have been totally buried in the mud banks - all you could see was this eye. I mean, they were so well camouflaged that you would never know a croc was there until he moved or attacked."

I asked George about Sweetheart, his views ideas and any encounters he might have had with the infamous rogue.

"Well", he said "I did go down with Ranger Dave Lindner to try and catch Sweetheart. It was the same time as the Willesee television crew were there trying to film it. We did see Sweetheart one night, we were trying to net it, but that old croc was plenty smart, he just swam along parallel with the net, never went into it. We also tried to get him to attack us, it was funny really. Here was this procession out on the river, Dave and I in one boat trying to get a crazy croc to attack us and right behind us was this boat full of television people, cameras etcetera hoping to film it!" laughed George.

"Thoughts came to me of what might have happened had Sweetheart decided to attack the media boat instead! That would have been a real circus."

"Anyway nothing worked while I was there - we hung around the areas of attack just trying to goad him into showing himself," continued George "We tried hooks baited with flying fox, we even

tried a trap with another croc as bait, but it appears Sweetheart was just too cunning."

I asked George what in his opinion made a croc like Sweetheart go rogue.

"He was probably just a problem croc", he said. "Maybe he had a confrontation with a man and boat at some time, probably he found out that he was boss in the water. As I said before crocs are like people, they are different with different personalities so it's hard to say what made him go off. Certainly they do become excited when there is thrashing about in the water, like when there is a fish fighting or animals in the water. I don't know", he said. "Maybe he just didn't like boats!"

Chapter 11

"POKE THE RIFLE DOWN HIS THROAT & GIVE IT BOTH BARRELS"

Denver Marchant

The situation with Sweetheart now had deteriorated to the position where there was no longer a choice. He had to be removed one way or the other. Fishermen had got the message that to fish here was to invite disaster. Ranger Dave Lindner was despatched to solve the problem before someone lost their life and the government was placed in a very embarrassing predicament. As with most others familiar with Sweets, Dave became attracted to the area and was not adverse to exploring during his free time.

Ranger Lindner invited Northern Territory police, CIB Detective Denver Marchant to assist him in the removal of the troublesome croc. Denver picks up the story.

"Dave invited me down to the Finniss basically to give him a hand I suppose", he said. "The whole object was we were going to shoot it. It wasn't an issue to catch it, that had been tried before and failed. Dave provided the artillery for the trip which consisted of a .375 Holland and Holland. There's a bit of history to that as a matter of fact - it was one of Donald Campbell's guns. It had a scope mounted on it and the idea was that if we got a long shot we could bowl the croc over with that. He also had a very short barrelled .557 double rifle. The trick was to entice this thing into attacking the boat and then poke the rifle down its throat and give it both barrels. Try and take its mind off things for a while! " he laughed. "And of course I had my .357 handgun strapped on my hip."

"Who was going to hold the rifle?" I enquired.

"Well, I was going to do the shooting" said Denver. "Dave was going to drive the boat."

"We set up camp and I'm not too sure if we spotted the croc the first day or not. Certainly it was either the first day or the second. We saw him about 150 metres away. That's at a guess. It

emerged and swam parallel to us, up at the top end of Sweets. I got a chance to get a good look at it then and I thought 'My God, it is quite some croc.' You could see a fair bit of it out of the water There was a light wind blowing and it was just too far for an accurate shot. We thought, 'to hell with that, that's crazy'. So that night we went back out again with the object of goading it into attacking the boat. We desperately wanted to get it. All sorts of things had been tried to date, without success. We set up a couple of croc traps, two had already been set previously by Rangers that had been down there. There were a couple of snares too. We chopped down a half a tree and made a neat little access to it. We baited a couple of those with big hocks of buffalo we had knocked over earlier in the day. It was pretty good, a well set up trap. In theory it should have worked quite well but looking at the size of Sweetheart now it just wouldn't have worked at all. We might have got its front end in the trap and that's about all.

We came out at about 5.30 to 6.00 pm and cruised all over the place. Firstly to a place directly across from the landing, where Dave thought the croc had a bit of a haunt. It used to centralise most of its attacks from that area. I believe one of the attacks (Brian Cowan's attack, chapter 7) was directly in this area.

What we were doing was stopping and starting the motor, trying to reproduce situations that had invited previous attacks. The croc obviously had some sort of a thing about outboard motors. Nothing worked, we didn't even get a glimpse of it that day. We stayed out until fairly late at night, probably approaching 9 o'clock. I was casting the occassional lure and just before it became totally dark, I snagged up on a branch. We must have been in about six foot of water and so I just thought 'Damn it, I'll just snap it off'. But not Dave. He yelled 'No, no, I'll get it'. I said to him,

Top photo - Author - 17 ft croc takes a Magpie
Goose

Photo Bill Green, University Sydney

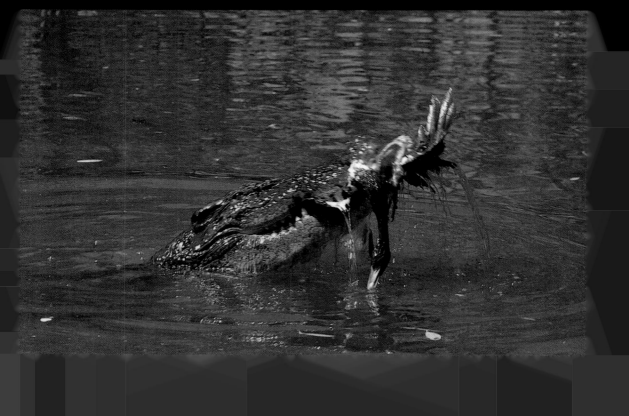

'Don't be ridiculous, this is crazy.' But he insisted. 'No, no, she's right' he said.

As he lunged into the murky water I made a grab for the back of his pants. He popped up shortly afterwards with my $5 lure and threw it casually down into the bottom of the boat. I said, 'Hell Dave, you're crazy!' I mean, we had only just seen this huge croc. But he just drawled 'No, it'll be up the other end of the waterhole. No worries. She's sweet'. Meanwhile, he's standing there dripping water all over the place. He didn't dive overboard but he had the whole top of his body submerged to retrieve the lure. His head and shoulders were certainly well under the water. I don't know if Dave recalls that or not, but I recall it quite vividly" laughed Denver.

"It was no big deal for Dave. Anyway it was around 9 o'clock and it was particularly dark. Dave was stopping and starting, reversing etc and so I called to him. 'If this thing grabs us while we are reversing we are going to go straight under the drink!' Dave just looked at me and said 'Oh yeah, yeah'. At that stage we were fairly convinced we weren't going to have any contact or incident that night so to speak. I had this double barrelled rifle I had been nursing, so I put it down. I had no sooner grabbed hold of the side of the boat than Dave flicked the motor into forward gear and it started to move."

"I was looking at him when suddenly there appeared this hideous apparition behind him. I wasn't really sure what was going on, for a minute or two. I was just watching him when the boat went...bang! Dave shot forward, landing on his knees, I fell over backwards. I could just make out the tail end of this monster. It was the croc right up at the top of the outboard motor. Of course, water just poured in everywhere as Dave yelled out 'Croc'! I used some far more colourful language myself."

"I suppose it happened in a second, like most things that scare the pants off you but it seemed to take ages. I don't have any recollection of seeing teeth as such, I could just see Dave with something huge and black behind him. It was pitch dark and we never had a torch or lantern switched on at the time. The whole idea was just to make this thing attack the boat, stick the gun down its throat and give it both barrels. Which, incidentally was Dave's plan. I certainly wouldn't have planned things that way but Dave was calling the shots and he kept saying 'This'll work, this'll work!' I was a bit apprehensive about it working anyway. I think even Dave had second thoughts about it too. I mean, I was holding the double rifle pretty close to

him and a .577 going off in close proximity like that would render him fairly deaf for a while."

"There was this huge black shape behind him. Dave obviously couldn't see it. But he could see my face. My eyes must have enlarged to the size of dinner plates. This would have given him a bit of a shock too. We both fell base over apex in the boat, as water came hurtling over the stern. The croc actually pulled the transom right under and water just poured in everywhere."

"For a split second we were absolutely paralized. We just sort of looked at each other. We knew what had happened, there was no two ways about that. Of course, the motor just stopped with sheer fright. Obviously it got a severe shock as well. I gingerly picked up the gun as Dave put the spot light on but there was nothing to see. Sweetheart had broken off the engagement."

"We stayed in that area and shone the light everywhere but there wasn't a movement. You couldn't even hear a bird - it was a terribly eerie feeling. When he hit mate, he sure hit hard but it all happened so fast. There was an almighty great thump, a hell of a shake and it was over. It obviously had hold of the top of the outboard motor, that's what it did. Dave has photos of that. He came directly at the back of the boat, at the top of the outboard motor. That's where it all occurred. When we had a look at the outboard motor we could see where the teeth had hit it and dragged it down. We had just started to move forward and obviously the croc misjudged or it would have pulled the boat straight under. There's no doubt about that. It hit the tip of the cowling. I could see this black shape behind and it looked enormous, absolutely terrifying. It so scared me that my bum bit a chunk out of the seat and I left crimp marks where I was trying to hang on. Water went everywhere as this thing fell back into the river with an almighty splash. The force just propelled the boat forward."

"When we put the light on a couple of minutes later, there was just dead calm, you couldn't hear a thing. We put the light over the side and we could see bubbles rising up beside the boat. I thought, 'This is charming, the thing is sitting right underneath us.' I suggested to Dave that it might be a good idea if we went for a run. I think the first words I spoke were pirated straight from the movie Jaws. 'Hell, we need a bigger boat'. There was no doubt about it - the croc was much bigger than the boat we were in which measured twelve feet."

"Of course Dave insisted on having a look around with the spot light. But there was no way the croc was going to oblige us by coming up while the light was on and we didn't see it again that night at all. Unfortunately I had to start work again the following day and I don't mind admitting that I was rather keen to do just that."

"The little expedition to grab this croc wasn't all that flash", he laughed.

I asked Denver how long after Dave had been in the water to retrieve the lure did the croc attack.

"About ten minutes", he said. "Certainly no more".

"We were right in the middle of the river. We had made all sorts of little plans if we were attacked and the boat was turned over. The way I worked it out, it seemed pretty inevitable that we might end up in the drink with the thing. I said, 'Look they are your guns Dave and I'm not about to dive for them with that croc there'. He said, 'No, we'll be right, we'll be right!' 'The main thing is that you stay with the boat, stay with the boat!'

"That's pretty good advice I suppose", continued Denver. "I had seen first hand quite a few incidents of crocodiles, the legacy of what they can do. I'd been involved in a few little encounters when I spent three years over at Gove. I saw what a four gallon drum looked like after being crunched up by one. An aboriginal lady was taken over there. She was quite horrificly chewed up, there's no two ways about that. Grim stuff! The advice to stay with the boat though, I thought 'Dave, like hell. I know what I'm going to do. I'm going to sprint for the bank flat strap.' Dave was carrying a bit of weight but with his wide feet he could motor along through the water fairly well. I couldn't see much sense in staying with the boat. Fortunately, I didn't have to. When the water came in the boat, and there was an enormous amount in there (I'd say the boat was half full.")

"Dave certainly had a narrow escape, the croc's teeth would have only missed his arm by centimetres. There's no doubt about that, they would have been right on him. It was only sheer good luck that we didn't go completely underwater because just a split second before we had been reversing. We had to bail a lot of water out before we got back to camp, fortunately the motor appeared only too pleased to start. It did take quite a few pulls to kick it over and I had visions of a repeat performance. Needless to say, I had hold of the gun pretty firmly at that stage of the game.

"We were shaken by the attack, perhaps me more so than Dave. Afterall, I had seen it face to face first hand, while he had his back to it, watching my reaction. He certainly would have seen white eyes and teeth, no doubt about that", he laughed.

"Definitely not recommended to soothe the nerves", he mumbled. "No, not at all".

D. Lindner using a dead croc for bait for Sweetheart

Outboard motor showing signs of the scars from Sweetheart's massive teeth - Photo D. Lindner

A collection of huge croc skulls - Photo D. Lindner

Freshwater croc taking fisherman's lure

The ⁂ News

Giant crocodile scare:
TWO BOATS SUNK!

By DAVID PROUNCE

TWO Territory Parks and Wildlife Commission officers will act as bait to catch a large saltwater crocodile terrorising fishermen on the Finniss River.

'WE WILL BE THE BAIT'

Sweetheart and his Finniss River home that he
defended so vigorously - N.T. Museum

Chapter 12

MEDIA REPORT

Dave Lindner

Photo - Author

Darwin, June, AAP ---- A 17 foot rogue crocodile which stalks and attacks outboard motors at a popular fishing spot south of Darwin is defying all attempts to capture or kill him.

The huge saltwater crocodile has attacked dozens of dinghies at Sweetmans Lookout on the Finniss River, about 80 kilometres south east of Darwin. The rangers, led by crocodile expert David Lindner of the Northern Territory Parks and Wildlife Service were hunting the crocodile and were prepared to shoot him.

They had not sighted him and were ready to abandon the search when he loomed out of the murky water and clamped his jaws around the rear of the boat.

A spokesman for the Service said the crocodile shook the dinghy savagely, and let go only to take a bite at the outboard motor. He then submerged and disappeared.

The rangers were hunting the big croc following an attack two days earlier on a fishing expedition.

Mr Lindner and a Darwin CIB Detective, Sergeant Denver Marchant, were fishing for barramundi on a day off when they were attacked.

"The crocodile surfaced without warning and bit the top off the motor", Mr Lindner said. "He disappeared before we could do anything about it. I wouldn't say I was frightened - I was more interested than frightened", he said.

"I understand his motives, but I suppose the average bloke out fishing would see him as a jaws-type monster".

The Wildlife Service spokesman said the aggressive crocodile had attacked the boat of a safari operator in March, and had been responsible for a series of attacks on fishing dinghies last year. He said rangers wanted to capture the crocodile but were prepared to shoot him if all attempts to do so continued to fail.

Rangers were camped at the spot trying various methods - including using other dead crocodiles as lures, tape recordings of territorial roars of crocodiles and sonic equipment to drive him into nets.

"We would like him alive for research purposes". the spokesman said. "We want to know why he is so aggressive towards outboard engines".

"Our theory is that he associates the sound of the engines with the roar of a crocodile trying to assert a claim on his territorial patch".

The spokesman said there was no doubt the crocodile was clever.

"It's extremely evasive - the most evasive crocodile we've struck", he said.

"He's never seen on the surface in daylight, he won't be drawn into a spotlight at night, and he doesn't bask on the banks of the river because there are no basking tracks.

Most crocodiles can be captured or shot at because they can be approached discreetly. But not this fellow. He submerges until he attacks and then he just looms out of the water.

Plenty of other crocs have been seen on the Finniss but they're not our fellow because they're not big enough. He's really a wily one."

The spokesman said the 17 foot length and six foot width of the rogue crocodile had been established by sighting reports and by measurements of teeth-marks on the outboard motor of the Wildlife dinghy attacked last Saturday.

He said the crocodile was about 40 years old, and had survived through the hunting seasons of the fifties and sixties because of his cunning.

"He must have been a big croc even then, and to escape the hunters he had to be clever", he said.

The crocodile had to be dealt with, the spokesman said, because he represented a potential danger to human life and because a tourist safari boat regularly passed through Sweetmans Lookout.

"I hope we don't have to shoot him", he said. "He could prove to be invaluable as research material if we were able to capture and move him to another spot."

"We'd also like to use him in any future crocodile breeding farm experiments".

The spokesman said the crocodile had attacked an aluminium dinghy at the fishing spot last September and had overturned it, forcing the two occupants to swim for shore.

"But we are certain he is not attacking under predatorial instincts, but territorial", he said.

E. Jacko ·86·

Chapter 13

THE CAPTURE - "NOW COME ON SWEETHEART"

Dave Lindner

By now it was obvious Sweetheart's days were numbered. Ranger Dave Lindner had been assigned to the case and in the tradition of the Canadian Mounties - he always got his "man".

Lindner was probably the Wildlife Department's most experienced croc expert, having captured live, troublesome or rogue crocs on many occassions. Dave is a quiet, unassuming type of fellow but knows the bush like few men in the north. In his ranger days he was the scourge of barramundi poachers, illegal netters and croc shooters, bringing many of them to justice.

"The live capture part of the action against Sweetheart was really only part of what was going on", he said. "We had attempted on occassions to kill him, in fact the second attack on the 9th June was to patrol the billabong and invite an attack. This was to be followed up by shooting the animal, while he was attacking us.

Another time we hung a dog or a dingo in clear view of the opposite bank. It was close to the place where we eventually caught him in the live trap and the dog was kept under constant surveillance by a sniper. At one stage Sweetheart did come out and seize hold of the bait, unfortunately for us, the chap in charge of the operation had handed the sniping position over to a younger person, not familiar with firearms certainly not experienced enough for this type of shooting and he missed.

The encounter took place early in the morning, Sweetheart had approached very cautiously, he was a cagey old croc. The sniper was nestled in the fork of a tree right opposite the bait and he only saw a glimpse of the eyes and nostrils protruding above the water. Certainly not much to shoot at, and so he quickly drew a bead and fired. The distance was probably a good 200 yards and the bullet whistled cleanly over the monster croc's head and smacked harmlessly into a big old Leichardt tree. Actually the fellow thought he had hit him and so we searched for a long time, but eventually I located the spent slug embedded in a tree, about two feet too high. As I say, it was about a 200 yard shot, but with a Brno .308 complete with heavy barrel. The rifle was plenty accurate enough to make the shot. The objective

was to kill the animal, but at the same time we did have live traps set as they offered the croc a chance to go to a bait without the risk of human interferance.

We also baited hooks, the traditional method for catching crocs, large specimens in particular. When the animal takes the hook it subsequently fights the line and invariably wrecks its insides to the point where it cannot survive.

We did set up a boat for tourist use too. We gave it to "The Last of the Wild Safaris" operators. It was a large boat, heavy with a double skinned bottom which had been used for offshore fishing, the bottom had cracked and a new one had been welded in. It was a very solid dinghy, 14 to 15 feet long and quite capable of sustaining a croc attack without being tipped over. The understanding we had with the company was for them to use only this boat in the billabong, and not use their light weight punts. Unfortunately a fishing competition had been scheduled and it looked like attracting about a dozen boats, most likely the light—weight car top types. If Sweetheart attacked one of these, well, I think everyone acknowledged that eventually one of the croc attacks would result in a fatality, regardless of how innocent the croc's intentions might have been. In that case the wildlife authorities would have been placed in an awkward position.

So we had a priority......get rid of Sweetheart! It was very disheartening because the very reason I provided the heavy boat to the safari operators was recognition of Sweetheart's right to exist and inhabit the billabong. People should have adapted their fishing practices to accomodate him" said Dave.

"However, we had not been able to get the public to support Sweetheart, in fact, generally speaking they were amused bystanders to the whole thing. We realised that should an attack take place, resulting in a fatality, we would very quickly be on the brunt of a public backlash. That was something we couldn't afford. If you lose your job on one croc project that blows up, you can no longer help others. Unfortunately for Sweetheart, there was no pressure that he be recognised as an identity, nor was there any pressure from having people stopped from doing the very things that make them vulnerable to such an attack", he said.

So the stage was set for Sweetheart's demise, it would soon be over. His days of cruising as king of the billabong were definately drawing to a close. In fact, the wheels of fortune were already firmly turning to rid Sweets Lookout of the giant crocodile. From now on there would be no turning back.

The actual trap set by the rangers was a mechanical noose, a lassoo type affair, a simple mundane gadget, certainly an unfitting end to such a magnificent identity as Sweetheart. Sweetheart, the king of Sweets Lookout, unvanquished victor of numerous encounters with metal boats, Sweetheart whose awesome size and appearance was forever etched into the memories of many Top End fishermen, Sweetheart the saurian who had effectively foiled every attempt to capture, trap or shoot him to date - outsmarting the best man could pit against him - now calmly swam towards his death. Unaware of his date with destiny, the giant croc seized hold of the dangling bait and in one gut rendering, wrenching lunge, tore flesh from the carcass. The force released the trigger mechanism of the spring loaded arm, causing it to fly upwards and jerking the snare taut. It was all over - Sweetheart's freedom was a thing of the past.

Sweetheart was probably unaware that he had in fact been captured, the snare gently easing over his

massive body to lodge firmly behind the shoulder blades, as the croc moved backwards into the security of his river home. Gradually the broad industrial belting (chosen so as not to cut or choke the croc) began to tighten around the massive armoured girth. A sad end for a formidable foe, a humiliating defeat for this formerly undefeated king of the river, to fall victim to nothing more than a whip pole snare. Given the choice, I am confident the old rogue would have preferred to end his days the very way he had lived - as king of the waterhole - if not, then at least to die with the dignity of mortal combat with old adversaries, the metal boats that invaded his domain.

"I had set the trap with Dave Higgins" said ranger Dave. "It had been set several weeks earlier, but not baited. We didn't pull it out as we felt it was better to have the croc get used to the device in the area . I had this week off and we had gone to Sweets Lookout on a private shooting trip. On this particular day I was standing right opposite the point, where we later set the trap, with three other fellows - Alan Morten, Geoff McDonald and Buck Salau. Buck, a very observant bloke, suddenly yelled out 'Look at that stick, it's moving!' He

was referring to an object in the middle of the billabong. I said 'That's not a stick, that's a croc, it's Sweetheart.' 'He must be hungry, he's looking at us'. Let's bait the trap we might get him'.

"I had picked up a dead dingo on the side of the road coming into Sweets, so we used it for bait. It had been hit by a vehicle and proved the ideal bait too, in fact, it was almost like an omen of success to find something so ideal, as conveniently as that" said Dave.

And so Sweetheart did the rest there in the early half light of daybreak over the beautiful Finniss River, driven by hunger, the giant croc eased stealthily, warily towards his date with death. An egret screeched into startled flight as Sweetheart lunged forward from the murky depths, clamping its fearsome jaws firmly onto the dingo's carcass. The trap was sprung. The broad noose playing out sufficient line like an angler playing a giant fish on a fishing reel. The idea behind the noose or snare was to act like a giant shock absorber. It gives and does not resist the intense action of a struggling crocodile. As the animal fights, or lays back on the noose, it gives way in a degree of response to the pressure applied. Crocs have a limited capacity for sustained, intense action and these bouts must be interspersed with frequent intervals of rest, otherwise the saurian quickly succumbs or exhausts itself.

Unlike an encounter with man or animal, the contest with the snare was a foregone conclusion. Afterall, the trap was designed to exploit the croc's weakness rather than oppose its incredible strength. Sweetheart mustered and brought to bear all the available resources of a three quarter ton, five metre plus, crocodile. The powerful jaws, wicked teeth, thrashing, powerful tail and awesome speed, any of which would be capable of destroying a natural enemy, now proved useless against the snare. In keeping with its kind, Sweetheart fought a series of short, intense bouts.

By now he had lost all interest in eating, the ravaged dingo hung forlornly overhead gently swaying in a slight breeze. Sweetheart, by contrast, was totally engrossed in his bid for freedom. Enraged, frightened, and frustrated by the restricting bands of the snare, the croc struck out blindly at the unseen enemy. Who was this enemy that held him bound and captive, who would dare to challenge the legendary king of the waterhole? Where was it?

All night long the saurian rolled, lurched, lunged, wrenched, thrashed, slashed and struck at its mechanical adversary. Hour after hour his fighting force slowly ebbed away, his powerful grunts gradually subsiding to muted snorts of defiance. By early morning light the broad noose was still firmly

How Sweetheart met her death

SWEETHEART, the lady with the flashing teeth and sparkling eyes, is dead, but her memory will linger on.

A few will remember Sweetheart for her not-so-playful life-bites.

And many will secretly admire her well-proportioned body when it is displayed in the $6 million museum planned for Darwin.

Courtesy N.T News

Sweetheart, of course, was the name given by Wildlife rangers to the 780kg and 5.1 metre-long crocodile which had been biting into fishing boats for several months.

Territory and Wildlife Commission officers, who caught the monster in a trap last week, brought Sweetheart into Darwin yesterday.

And it's probably just as well she was caught because Australian Safaris of Darwin are running a fishing competition on Show weekend in the area where Sweetheart was caught.

Sweetheart last attack on a barramundi fisherman's dinghy was on July 15.

On that occasion Sweetheart varied her assault . . . previously she had attacked on or near the outboard motors in dinghies, but this time she attacked the bow.

So a trap was set. And at daylight — after five hours of work — four men retrieved Sweetheart from the trap and loaded her aboard a trailer for Darwin.

First they had to anaesthetise the croc and this took another 30 minutes.

But the injection took longer than usual to take effect and it was 1½ hours before she was sufficiently sedated to be towed away from the bank and across to a vehicle access landing.

However trouble struck from another quarter — a submerged log.

Sweetheart tangled with it and ingested a large quantity of water into its stomach.

She was still alive and breathing freely when loaded for transport to Darwin but though fluid was syphoned out of the windpipe Sweetheart did not respond.

Sweetheart, the terrible darling of Top End rivers died — but she'll be around (in less terrifying form) for a long time.

The mouth that defeated over 15 boats - Courtesy N.T. Museum

THE 300 YEAR CROC.

THE OLD CROC. CROAKS

Sweetheart the 780kg, 5.1 metre motor boat munching crocodile has meet a watery end.

Boat croc's biting days over

A 5.10 metre crocodile which had terrorised fishermen in the Sweets lookout area is dead.

It was caught yesterday by a team from the Territory Parks and Wildlife Commission.

The team set out to catch the crocodile after its latest attack on a dinghy on Saturday.

It was decided it would have to be caught because it was a menace to people fishing in the area.

The crocodile weighed 780 kilograms.

The crocodile died five hours after being caught because it was accidentally trapped in logs floating in the lagoon.

It was under anaesthetic, and swallowed too much water.

The crocodile's skin and skeleton will be displayed in the Darwin museum.

At the moment scientists are dissecting it and looking into any information that may help in understanding crocodiles.

Monster In Death Trap

Photo courtesy N.T.News

in place around his ample armoured girth - Sweetheart faced his last sunrise.

Dave Lindner rose early that morning, stretched and yawned. It was half light and little stirred on the eerie calm over the river as he strode toward the trap site.

"I approached the snare from the far side of the billabong" he said. "Everything looked in order right up until the big croc rolled over and broke the surface with a huge splash. Sweetheart was hooked!" he exlaimed to me.

Dave's heart began to pound in his ears as he raced back to the camp to alert his assistants. Soon the group were assembled around the snared form of the giant croc.

"Hell, he is enormous!" said one as the big saurian rolled and thrashed about in the water before him.

Now came the interesting part, the securing of the big fellow with ropes and the administering of the sedative. Although routine enough, this was to be the first time any of the group had tangled with a croc as large as Sweetheart. Dave related the story to me.

"First we secured the top jaw with a rope using a long pole, mainly because it's easy to loop under the teeth", he said.

"We just secured the head by tying it to something then we threw a rope around the bottom jaw, put a second loop over the top one and pulled the mouth closed. Once we had his business end secured he was history. Looking back at what we knew about crocodile handling then and the fact that we didn't have a suitable facility set up to accommodate a croc of this size, the best option would have been for it to remain in the waterhole. The second option, was what actually happened - the animal died.

A near maximum amount of research material was retrieved from the croc - the stomach contents, the gonads (which deteriorate very quickly after death) showed the animal was still sexually active and not a senile animal in any way. Crocs have certain none renewing organs, such as the eye lens which deteriorate the same as they do in humans. It is therefore unlikely that a crocodile will ever live for 300 years. There is no need for this in corcodile population survival, and it would be very difficult for them to exist that long with such deterioration in crucial organs. So it's my guess that Sweetheart was over forty and under eighty years of age, something like that. There may be more precise information on ages available from the people who work full time in crocodile research.

It was known even then that such animals over five to six feet long are difficult to handle and keep alive after capture. The reason for this is the build-up of lactic acid in muscles due to the stress it undergoes from the constant handling. The lactic acid essentially has a shock effect and can result in death. Under laboratory conditions crocodiles have been stressed until they died, then comparitive studies have been made of the muscles of un-stressed specimens.

The Rhodesians have proved that if you hit a croc with a successful anaesthetic (they use Flaxadil) which knocks the specimen out quickly, lactic acid build-up is minimised.

However the problem was that they didn't have dosage rates which allowed for beasts the size of Sweetheart, so we had to use theoretical dosage rates. Unfortunately they didn't work well enough and it did contribute to Sweethearts early death. Under Flaxadil animals are no longer under stress, so you can keep them peaceful until they can be relocated to suitable surroundings. Usually too, animals such as this carry injuries from fish spines, fighting etc which would normally heal quickly in the wild but become infected when the beast is subjected to prolonged stress as occurs early after capture. Injuries can become gangrenous and even fatal, even if the croc survives the initial stress of the capture. But Sweetheart drowned, it's as simple as that. He wouldn't have even suffered from stress that would have taken some hours to happen" said Lindner.

"It's a pity too, he was a perfect specimen of a large crocodile. It is a common problem when handling crocs, they have a number of valves in their respiratory system which automatically close to stop them taking water into their lungs. These valves are de-activated by anaesthetic, before the animal becomes unconscious. So naturally they just have to be kept out of water while affected by drugs. In Sweetheart's case, he was active, difficult to handle, right up until we got him trussed up with ropes. He kept spinning around against the captive ropes, in fact the ones around his snout looked as if they were cutting through. We had used several lots of ropes due to his size. I left the original capture sling around his shoulders accordingly and the retaining steel cable that tethered the sling to the river bank. It added security as we towed him out with the boat. (The croc had to be towed back to the camp side of the river). We had his head tied to the stern of the boat and as we took off, the sling was let loose and snagged underwater on a huge log. It was a massive tree right in the middle of the billabong. Actually we thought the pulling against the boat was Sweetheart's own dead weight. I mean, he was a big boy, but in fact he was snagged. Naturally this started to pull the boat's stern and the crocodile under the water. Once we realised the problem I dived overboard and tried to unhook the rope. By that time you can understand that he could have taken a lot of water.

We finally got him free and towed him back across the river to the trailer parked at Sweets Landing. At this stage the croc was still breathing and the drug was starting to take effect, so we quickly hauled him out of the water and up onto the trailer. He just lay there with his head down" continued Dave.

I asked how one might raise a three quarter ton crocodile out of a jungle river and onto a trailer.

"We put a number of bands around his body and winched him up" said Dave. "As well as that we had four good strong men lifting, each was probably good for 200 lbs under those circumstances. With them all lifting, we slowly used the Tirfor Winch to winch him onto the trailer. We used two winching points, one behind the shoulder, the other behind the back legs.

We used industrial belting, the wide stuff, so that he would not be injured in any way.

At this stage I noticed water running from his mouth and I feel he was taking water down his windpipe. As I pointed out before, these valves normally operate automatically, in fact crocs are like buffalo, if you throw water on their nose their nostrils instantly snap shut. But because of the drug, the valves weren't operating. He took water into his lungs and probably drowned very quickly.

We did try to save him by siphoning to clear the water. We used a half inch rubber hose and poked it down his gullet but it was no use. Really you need something very, very soft, pliable and very well lubricated for that sort of job", he said looking a little dejected.

Suddenly it was all over, the story had ended. Sweetheart, terror of boats and men was dead. The creature from Sweets lagoon was gone.

Suprisingly as it seems, despite the numbers of attacks the big croc successfully launched on boats and motors, no loss of life occurred. I asked Dave if he regarded it as a little "miraculous" that no fatality had taken place.

"Not really" he answered. "I don't believe Sweetheart was out after people, he wasn't a maneater, however he also wasn't a non-maneater. But his attacks were not inspired by predatory instincts at the time. No, I don't find that a problem at all. I think people could have contributed to a fatal attack through panic. Take those chaps that were spilled into the water at night, one swam over the top of the other. When they hit the bank one of them swam right through a clump of Pandanus leaves and got about 700 prickles in him. Of course this is a pretty normal reaction to such a horrifying thing. If you think of all the people who would have hung over the side of a boat hundreds of times, retrieving fish and he never hit any of them. All the opportunities he had to take men were never acted on. Not once! But he did home right in on slow or starting outboard motors.

There was enough natural feed in that billabong to feed plenty of crocs. I would say that billabong would have been home to hundreds of crocs originally. The only limit would have been those Sweetheart tolerated - kicking the bigger crocs out. But there would have been plenty in their burrows on the outskirts of the swamp i.e. rival males. They would have been dispersed because of the aggression from their peers. At the time we pursued Sweetheart the habitat there carried 95 freshwater crocs and at least 10 salties, possibly 15. It would have probably carried 200 adult salties. Yeah, plenty of tucker for them" he said.

"We are finding now that crocs are dispersing everywhere under territorial aggression. We see them in small holes etc where they have been pushed out by bigger crocs", he said.

In the old days bush people would have killed these for food. One thing intrigued me about the giant croc and that was how he came to be saddled with the unlikely title of "Sweetheart". I mean, a more less accurate title could scarcely be found. so I asked Dave who gave the title to the old fellow.

"I did" he said smiling as he said it. "After the attack with Denver Marchant the name just occurred to me. Denver was a well known CIB detective, good at handling bad criminals - a tough man. Denver, generally when he was collaring someone used to address them "Now come on Sweetheart." his affectionate way of handling troublesome types. So I thought with Denver being involved, seeing him, not exactly frightened, but powerless, unable to handle a bit of aggression and all this taking place at Sweets Lookout, well the name Sweetheart just seemed to fit. So I gave him the name. Up till this time the crocodile was unnamed, just the big croc at Sweets. I thought that Sweetheart just fitted him. If it had been anywhere else I wouldn't have called it Sweetheart", he said.

Sweetheart's body now made the long, dusty haul back to Darwin on the back of the trailer, where he was finally mounted and shipped all over the country as a featured exhibit. Eventually the specimen came to its final home - the Darwin Museum where some 120,000 visitors a year file past in silent awe of the giant from Sweets Lagoon.

"In the case of the Sweetheart exhibit, there is a complete mounted specimen and a skeleton standing alongside it. Obviously the original skull is in Sweetheart's skin, while the skull on the skeleton is from a 16 foot 10 inch croc which was shot at Point Stuart on the floodplains below Jimmys Creek. The croc had the jaw broken in two places by .303 bullets, although the healing process was already under way but the animal couldn't eat with a broken jaw and it starved to death. Most of the skeleton is that of Sweetheart", he said.

I asked Dave his views on the size of saltwater crocodiles.

"I don't believe in any croc over twenty three feet" he said. "Other authorities allow for specimens up to twenty six feet but to me that is an enormous crocodile. It's hard to imagine. There are plenty of Sweethearts around today, not hundreds but there are probably a dozen or more that size in the South Alligator, some in the Adelaide, Daly, the Mary system, the Victoria etc. Certainly they are not rare and now shooting has ceased they will become increasingly common. Sweetheart was a typical monster croc" he said.

I asked Dave his ideas of what may have caused Sweetheart's dislike for boats and motors.

"I think it's the source of some sort of noise or triggering factor to bringing this territorial aggression or response from the crocodile" he said. "In this case the motor, particularly as it was in reverse. It may not be the way the croc hears it below surface. Certainly to our ears, above the water, it sounds just like the throaty, gurgling sound a crocodile makes when issuing a challenge or threat. It's not a roar at all - croc's don't roar. The roaring sound that people hear around waterholes is actually the great billed heron. Crocs don't roar, they just growl. People hear this deathly 'haaaaa' down in the swamp and immediately think - 'croc'. But really it's just a big old great billed heron wandering around calling to its mate. I have studied Greer's recordings of crocodile aggression noises, and they are a low burbling, gurgling, growl and to me anyway, it sounds similar to an outboard motor in reverse. In fact the attack Sweetheart made on me and Phil Hauser on the 9th June 1979 was carried out while we were actually reversing the boat. I remember saying to Phil at the time 'If my theory on reversing a motor is correct, we will go right down Sweetheart's gob!' and that's exactly what we did" said Dave.

"He didn't get the motor though, he missed and hit the transom, locked right onto it very firmly. The attack took place at 4.15 am and it was cold. Out of the blue there was this double bang at the stern of the boat and I lost my balance, consequently I couldn't use the .577 double rifle I had lying across my knees. The croc's snout was very close to me as he locked on and shook the boat. Phil Hauser took a tumble, rather heavily too, skinning his knees. Old Sweetheart really shook that boat! After a few seconds he released us, swam off and re-surfaced some fifty metres away. We were in a fairly solid boat so I had no worries. Actually I was interested in Sweetheart; he had become a bit of an obsession with me - an attractive obsession, rather than something of horror like he would have been to the people who were spilled into the water. They were still bug-eyed a week later!" laughed Dave.

"Phil was a bit less inclined towards crocs than me, he was in it for the adventure. He's a good man on crocs though. I remember one time we accidently ran right up the back of a big old croc in the Arafura Swamp. We were only in a fibreglass canoe. Phil got really annoyed with me that day, he maintained that I was concentrating more on the croc rather than getting away from it. 'You can stick that' was the way that he put it.

Sweetheart was a very aggressive male croc who was almost certainly responsible for at least eight out of the ten reported attacks to date. These attacks were mainly directed at burbling motors. It was almost certainly Sweetheart who was the culprit, it's extremely unlikely there would be two huge crocs of that size in the one waterhole. In a normal situation there is one large croc in a typical billabong. Now if that croc should leave, usually another specimen of similar size will move in - a croc with a totally different behaviour pattern. For example, when a seventeen foot three inch beauty was killed at the junction of the Wilton and Roper Rivers, a very aggressive, similar sized croc moved downriver and took its place and that happened almost immediately. Big crocs don't tolerate each other. I strongly believe that Sweetheart's attacks were motivated by his natural instincts to protect his territory against what he mistakenly saw as a rival. If he had been after people, he would have succeeded!. He would have taken people off the banks, out of boats etc.

The croc numbers were so depleted in that area that he may not have encountered another croc as large as himself for years. One other point worth mentioning is that Sweetheart had a damaged eye which could have been caused by an outboard. He also had chipped teeth and tops knocked off, probably also from outboard damage. His head bore some good scars too. Afterall, you can't chase outboard motors without wearing a little punishment into the bargain!

If he was hit in the head or the eye by such a motor, or even got a good dose of petrol in the eye, it would sour him. Certainly it wouldn't help his attitude towards boats and motors any!" he laughed.

"Maybe his bung eye contributed to the mistaken identity of boats. They are all maybe's of course" he said.

"One point you can be sure of however", he quipped looking at me with a erious expression. "If he had been out to kill people, believe me he would have succeeded!"

Photo State Reference Library - Croc in snare

Photo Dept. Chief Minister

Ferocious 'Sweety' preserved for all

SWEETHEART'S beguiling smile is something a lot of the Northern Territory Finniss River fishermen will long remember with a touch of the jitters.

The Sun, Monday, Sept. 15, 1980— Page 35

CROCODILE PROVOKED

THE "killer" crocodile responsible for the attack on two dinghies a week ago was probably provoked by the actions of the fishermen involved, a former croc-hunter believes.

Stefan Sebasten, who now operates a tourist safari company in Darwin, warned fishermen to leave the crocodiles alone.

He said people seeking a good photograph of a croc often chased one around with their dinghy, and many crocs suffered after being nicked by propellors.

"They don't give him any peace, he should be left alone. Crocodiles don't just go around snapping at anything," he said today.

"It is no wonder one could get angered enough to attack. I just want to warn these fishermen to leave the crocs alone."

Stefan said he gets to within a metre of the crocodiles every day while on tour, and even feeds some by hand.

In his days as a croc-hunter he used to drift along in an 11-foot dinghy, sleeping at night on board among the smelly bait, and never

had any attacks from crocs.

He believes the increase in the number of dinghies in the Territory has forced the croc out of his normal placid state.

But now with the bite taken out of the primitive leer, the smile may be remembered more sweetly by those that come eye to beady eye with the "magnificent" beast.

Sweetheart is the Territory's most famous crocodile.

He, despite the name, first made news several years ago when he chomped through a number of aluminium fishing dinghies in the Finniss River, about 75 km west of Darwin.

Today his reputation is more respectable as he takes his place among the rarities of the museum world.

Fourteen months of hard, dedicated work by three staff members of the Darwin Museum have seen that Sweetheart, aged about 70, is preserved for posterity.

The man behind the arduous task was Graeme Gow, the Museum's curator of Natural Sciences, connected to the vertebrate section.

Along with his assistant Paul Horner and highly-skilled taxidermist Ian Archibald he has restored Sweetheart to his pre-historic splendor.

"It was like a big jigsaw," said Graeme, describing the reconstructed skeleton.

He said there were no reference books telling how to totally reconstruct a crocodillian.

"It was a matter of trial and error," he said.

After the animal was skinned the body was cut into four sections and as much flesh trimmed off as possible.

The bones were then wired together and placed in water to allow the rest of the flesh to rot away by bacterial action.

During reconstruction the crocodile was shown to have had a few broken limbs.

"It's a bull crocodile," said Graeme, "and bull crocs are very territorial. I'd say the broken limbs were probably caused by fighting with other male crocodiles."

Graeme proudly said: "The animal is unique.

"It is certainly the largest skeletal mount and largest body mount of a crocodillian in any Australian museum and probably in any museum in the world."

Sweetheart got his name from a place called Sweet's Lookout, on Finniss River, which is a popular barramundi fishing ground with amateur fishermen.

It was in this area

From PAUL DOHERTY in Darwin

where his boat-eating escapades took place.

But there were never any crocodile tears, as Sweetheart had never shown a desire to become a man-eater.

Sweetheart was caught shortly before a public fishing competition in the Finniss River after one of his attacks.

The Territory Conservation Commission was worried he might get the desire just mentioned and so organised a party to snare him.

Sweetheart was trapped in a snare and anaesthetised.

But while being hauled towards the Commission's boat, the huge animal drowned.

That night the body was skinned, and four burly footballers helped the museum lads haul the skin and skull up the narrow stairs to the museum.

It took 20 minutes to climb the dozen or so steps with their load.

The skin was wrapped in plastic and put in a freezer until special tanks had been made to chemically treat it.

The skin has now been sewn on to a dummy body and fitted with specially made glass eyes from the United States.

Seeing the result is an awe-inspiring experience.

Sweetheart measures 5.1 metres in length, has a body girth of 3 metres and weighed in when caught at 780 kg.

For those wondering if Sweetheart was in fact a two-headed monster, Graeme explained:

"Sweetheart's skin and skull are complete on the body mount.

"The head on the skeleton came from an identical crocodile donated for the historic purpose by the Conservation Commission.

Because Darwin's museum is at present housed in temporary accommodation, Sweetheart is not yet on public display.

The new museum complex is due to be completed in July next year.

So Sweetheart's public debut will be in Melbourne this month at the Centenary Exhibition.

He will be flown south in a specially-made $1200 marine plywood case by RAAF Hercules.

Sweetheart has been valued at $50,000, but to Graeme, Ian, Paul and the people of Darwin he is priceless.

the Age - 20 September 1980

Photo courtesy N.T.News

I have always been just a little wary of the media myself, having experienced first-hand some exaggerations and biased stories by reporters. But certainly the Sweetheart story allowed the media to indulge in some absolute flights of fantasy.

"One television show won an award on their story and they never even saw the crocodile", said Dave Lindner.

Sweetheart was a celebrity, not only here in Australia but world-wide. In fact, I was living in the U.S.A. at the time of his capture and read the account in a Los Angeles newspaper.

"The releases given by the Wildlife service appeared in newspapers all around the globe" said Lindner. Immense interest was shown in the whole Sweetheart saga even if the truth was sometimes coloured

up a little.

Take this account from a British paper, under the heading:

THE 300 YEAR CROC

"She lived for 300 years. And even the kids find it hard to believe that the old croc has croaked at last. The astonishing monster - 20 feet and 136 stone - died as experts in Australia's far north tried to move her to a safer lagoon. They feared hunters might shoot her. Sweetheart, as the Aussies called her had an appetite to match her bulk. When her stomach was opened up yesterday, it revealed crunched human bones and two motorboat engines".

"I mean, 'crunched human bones and two motorboat engines' is fairy tale stuff even for much of the media. Not to mention the ultimate insult - Sweetheart was a male!" said Lindner.

Take this report from a Southern paper printed under the heading:

SWEETHEART FROM THE BLACK LAGOON
THE OLD CROC CROAKS

"Sweetheart - the giant crocodile who thrived on a diet of outboard motors - has chomped his last prop. The 5.5m, 780 kg reptile died as Northern Territory Wildlife Commission rangers were moving him to a more isolated area. Rangers estimate Sweetheart could have been up to 300 years old. His favourite pastime was to sneak up behind fishermen and bite the propellers off outboards or take a large piece out of the boats. He was credited with more than two dozen attacks."

Or how about this account also from a southern paper that had the 5.10m croc now grown to 7m.

ROGUE CROC IN HIDING

"Canberra - The Rum Jungle rogue - the 7 metre crocodile which has been terrorising NT fishermen has gone into hiding. The giant reptile has not been spotted since Tuesday when it was pursued by a party of hunters after it sunk two aluminium boats more than a week ago. That sighting was from a light plane being used by the hunters to try to determine the crocodile's movements. The crocodile was seen swimming cautiously and a good distance behind boats trolling live bait in a bid to lure it into the open. Four fishermen got the fright of their lives when the crocodile charged their small two-man boats in the Finniss River about 80 kms south east of Darwin. It seized the aluminium boats in its huge jaws, puncturing one boat and biting off part of an outboard motor. The hunting party has tried to lure the crocodile into the open long enough for a shooter to take aim but so far its efforts have been in vain. The hunters now have strung a net across the river in the hope the reptile will swim into it."

"You know a crocodile that has trouble distinguishing between a boat and another croc suddenly turns into a rogue crocodile who attacks outboard motors on sight", exclaimed Dave "A crocodile who had a turtle in its stomach, at the time of capture, now ends up having two outboard motors and human remains", he continued.

"A crocodile who had a turtle in its stomach, at the time of capture, now ends up having two outboard motors and human remains", he continued.

"When we cut up Sweetheart we found sections of aged wild pig in its stomach. Incidentally there is quite a story to that. I was out one day hunting flying fox for croc bait when I happened on this wild boar. I let go two shots from my shotgun, the shot straddling the pig and certainly hitting it in the shoulder. The boar leapt up upon the shot striking him, but within a few seconds went back to resuming its feeding. I was using No. 2 shot at the time and the remains of the wild pig we found in Sweethearts stomach also carried No. 2 shot. It was almost certainly the same pig, which either died or Sweetheart took him while wounded", he said.

"Sweetheart's stomach also contained bird remains, a complete long necked turtle and some barramundi".

Photo - Dept. Chief Minister
Sweetheart on Mike Walsh Show

Photo - Ian Archibald - Mounting Sweetheart

ATTACKS

1900's	Nugget Marjar
Nov. 1958	Croc shooter, Ray Petherick
1974	Attack on Boyne & Peter Litchfield & Dulcie Pattenden at midnight 30 yards from Sweets Landing
Oct. 1975	Half mile upstream - attack on Boyne again at 7 pm
Nov. 1975	Boyne, Richard Denton & Garry Jones - Sweetheart under boat
Nov. 1976	Report 17 ft croc at top end Sweets - Ken Phillips. Surfaced under boat, lifting boat right out of water
Sep. 1978	Max Curtain & Ian Watson - holed boat
Sep. 1978	Clyde Reborse - Station boat attacked at mooring
Sep. 1978	Mal Thomas & Kel Clarke
Sep. 15 1978	Brian Cowan & George Tsakissiris Punctured boat - swam ashore
Sep. 1978	Max Davidson - attack on boat
1979	Terry O'Brien - attack on outboard
1979	Carl Blumanis & Dick Gleissner Boat overturned
May 28 1979	Denver Marchant & Dave Lindner Attacked motor at 8.15 pm
June 9 1979	Dave Lindner & Phil Hauser - seized transom
1979	Sweetheart captured

SWEETHEART'S SPECIFICATIONS

Species - Saltwater Crocodile, Crocodylus Porosus

Length - 5.1m

Girth - 2.3m

Weight - 780kg

Snout/Vent Length - 2.45m

Distinguishing Features - Scars around head, damaged opaque eye, teeth chipped

Age - 40 to 80 years

Capture Date - 19 July 1979

Sex - Male

Testicles - Sexually active

Captured - Sweets Lookout, Finniss River, N.T.

SKULL MEASUREMENTS

Length - 65.5cm

Between Teeth Apertures - 5.4cm

Inter Occular - 7.2cm

Greatest Width - 46.5cm

Greatest Height - 32.00cm

Stomach Contents - Pig bones & bristles, two long necked turtles, parts of large Barramundi

MARCHANT & LINDNER ATTACK 1979

1976 ATTACK KEN PHILLIPS

EAGLES NEST

PHIL HAUSER & DAVE LINDNER ATTACK 9/6/79

2ND ATTACK BOYNE LITCHFIELD 197

1ST ATTACK ON BOYNE LITCHFIELD 1974

CROCS IN SWAMP
FLOATING GRASS
SWEETHEART TRAPPED, TOWED ACROS

LANDING

BRIAN COW SWIMMING INCI

MAX CURT & IAN WATS ATTACK SEPT. 1

ROAD

MAX DAVIDS ATTACK

ATTACK ON REBORSE BOAT

HOMESTEAD

Chapter 15

THE CAPTURE IN PICTURES

Dave Lindner

Good shot of Sweetheart being bound

Sweetheart's mouth
circle shows catfish spikes
embedded in mouth
Photo Ian Archibald

Sweetheart is manoeuvred to the river bank

Close ups of Sweetheart's head during winching

...Stages of being winched onto the trailer

Chapter 17

CONCLUSION

And so ends the Saga of Sweetheart.....or does it? The controversial rogue crocodile is as much in the public eye as ever.

After his capture and demise, the massive body was shipped to the Northern Territory Museum in Darwin where Dave Lindner and resident taxidermist, Ian Archibald, proceeded to remove the skin and mount it.

Today Sweetheart's new home in the museum is in a lifelike setting of his old home at "Sweets Lookout". According to the museum's Ian Archibald, Sweetheart would be the biggest attraction the facility maintains. Over 100,000 visitors a year flock to its modern setting overlooking beautiful Fannie Bay, many of them expressly to view the "rogue roc of Sweets Lagoon".

For some time after his capture Sweetheart travelled throughout the length and breadth of the nation.

saurian aboard trucks and planes and travelled to southern shows and exhibitions for all and sundry to view. Sweetheart even made a guest appearance on the Mike Walsh show in Sydney!

If you should wander into the museum one day chances are you will observe a group of tourists huddled around the massive figure of a crocodile. Yes - this is Sweetheart, still drawing sighs and gasps of amazement, still thrilling everyone who gazes upon his awesome frame.

Sweetheart may have expired, but my friend the legend lives on. So if you should find yourself on the waters of Sweets Look-out, Finniss River, some sultry evening, late in the Dry, be aware of the sights and sounds of the night as you paddle quietly along the beautiful, serene waterhole.

This is crocodile habitat - this was the battle ground. This is Sweetheart country!

PHOTO PAT CARRICK

ODE TO SWEETHEART

Sweetheart, Sweetheart, armoured giant
Great grey crocodile - you remained defiant
Until the end, you reigned supreme.
Throughout the years since the time of dream
Superb and awesome, frightening and bold
To all you encountered - terror untold
What shall we say, what shall we write?
Will history record your valiant fight?
Will it be one of survival, defence or attack
Which will it be, case of white or black?
The metal boats you did scathe and ravage
A hideous menace? A monster and savage?
Or maybe we misjudged your saurian ways
Perhaps you were protecting your billabong bays
Your river, your swampland, home through the ages
Let history judge your story on pages
Damage you did, there's no point denying
But the men folk did come Sweetheart defying
And so you attacked with violence rife
But to your credit, no loss of life
You matched your wit, fought and won
But then came hook, snare and gun.
Against these forces you had no hope
Man must reign, not look like a dope
Snared, roped, drugged - there you hung
So you died, trapped, alone and unsung
Drowned in your haunt with a pitiful sigh
Destroyed by the men you tried to defy
Sweetheart, Sweetheart will we mourn your passing?
In death, not life you have proven lasting.